HANDYMAN GARDENER

DAVID STEVENS

OCTOPUS BOOKS

Barbecue — see pages 22-3

Contents

Illustrations by

Paul Emra 48-77
Chris Forsey 2, 6-35
Sandra Pond 5
Paul Williams 36-46, 78-95

First published in Great Britain in 1984 by
Octopus Books Limited
a division of the Octopus Publishing Group
Michelin House, 81 Fulham Road,
London SW3 6RB

This edition published in 1989

© 1984 Octopus Books Limited
ISBN 0-7064-3883-3

Produced by Mandarin Offset
Printed and Bound in Hong Kong

INTRODUCTION

The first problem with do-it-yourself work of any kind is deciding the scope of one's activities. Many books on the subject seem to over-estimate the ambitions of the average do-it-yourselfer and make many projects needlessly complicated. One of the aims of this book will be to eliminate needless complexity from the various projects. If we can add to simplicity a soundness of construction and suitability to purpose we shall have the basis of good design.

We are concerned in this book with all the man-made elements of what we can regard as an outside room. First of all, there are structural features – paving, walls, fences, steps – to which can be added desirable features such as pools and patios. Then there are practical furnishings that include tables, chairs, lighting, built-in storage, sheds, and screens. To these may be added a variety of inessential but worthwhile items that help to give character to the 'hard landscape'. (All timber, unless otherwise specified, is of softwood.)

It is no longer the case that it is invariably cheaper to make-it-yourself than to buy. As it happens, it often is, but the great advantage of making anything with your own hands, within the limits of your practical ability, is that it answers your exact requirements – and of course, it is often far more satisfying to build something than to buy it off the peg.

SAFETY

The wise do-it-yourselfer is always concerned with safety, whether he is involved in a major project or a routine maintenance chore. This concern is doubly important if there are small children about the house. Always keep sharp edged tools – saws, chisels, planes, and so on – out of their reach. The same applies, of course, to chemicals such as paint strippers and pesticides. Never store such liquids in old drinks bottles.

Safety equipment will include goggles for use when you are cutting concrete or stone, a face mask if your work involves the raising of dust, and special gloves for bricklaying. You will be using ladders and steps for many of the jobs described in this book. Make sure they are in good condition, are properly secured when in use (especially on soft ground), and are stored away at night.

Electricity is potentially dangerous. If you are in the smallest doubt about DIY work in this field, consult a professional electrician. Use electrically powered tools with care: always unplug power drills, for instance, when changing drill bits.

However much care is taken, minor accidents such as cuts and grazes are bound to happen from time to time. Always keep a well-stocked first-aid kit in an accessible position.

LEVELLING The first jobs to tackle in a new garden are to establish levels and make sure the site is well drained.

Accurate levels can be found using home-made T-shaped boning rods. Align them at intervals down a slope, measuring the vertical differences between them. If building a terrace, use the 'cut-and-fill' principle, in which the excavated soil helps to build up the level immediately below it.

DRAINAGE If you have a problem of surface water, instal land drains to lower the water table. Lay 100 mm (4 in) diameter clay pipes in gravel-filled trenches sloping at a gradient of about 1 in 40 and ending in a soakaway. The pipes should be laid in a herringbone pattern (as shown) for maximum catchment, and the joints between pipes covered with pieces of slate, clay tile, or other impermeable material.

Whenever you are digging, remember to put the fertile topsoil to one side so that it can be used later.

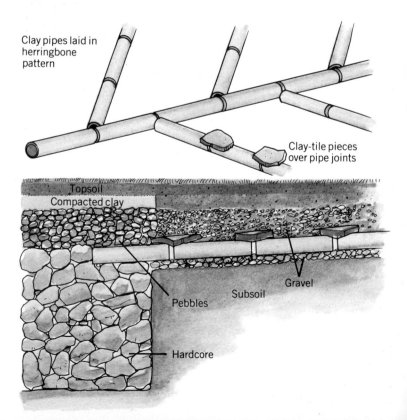

Clay pipes laid in herringbone pattern

Clay-tile pieces over pipe joints

Topsoil
Compacted clay
Pebbles
Subsoil
Gravel
Hardcore

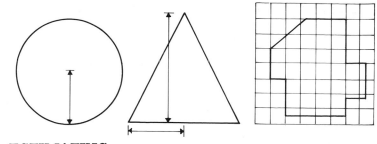

ESTIMATING You will save much money if you estimate
accurately the quantities of materials needed for a job.
Remember that the area of a square or rectangle is the length of
the base times the height; that of a triangle is half the length of
the base times the height; and the area of a circle is the square of
the radius times 3.14. You will need 50 bricks per square metre
of a 115 mm (4½ in) wall – one brick's width.

The chart below shows the amount of concrete to order. Find
the intersection of your area (horizontal) and thickness (radial)
lines and read off the volume vertically below. The vertical
volume line will give the amount needed of each ingredient of
two standard concrete mixes.

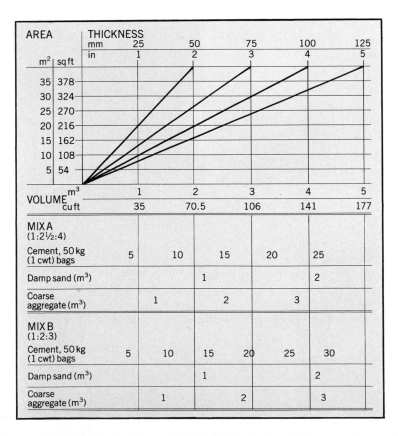

AREA	THICKNESS				
	mm 25	50	75	100	125
m² sq ft	in 1	2	3	4	5
35 378					
30 324					
25 270					
20 216					
15 162					
10 108					
5 54					
VOLUME m³	1	2	3	4	5
cu ft	35	70.5	106	141	177

MIX A (1:2½:4)						
Cement, 50 kg (1 cwt) bags	5	10	15	20	25	
Damp sand (m³)			1		2	
Coarse aggregate (m³)		1	2		3	

MIX B (1:2:3)						
Cement, 50 kg (1 cwt) bags	5	10	15	20	25	30
Damp sand (m³)			1		2	
Coarse aggregate (m³)		1		2		3

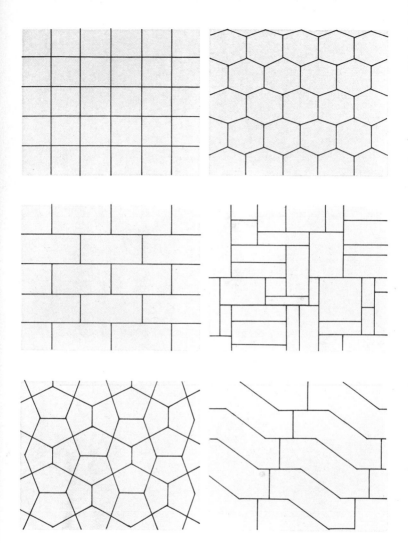

PAVING SLABS Precast-concrete paving slabs come in a great many shapes, sizes, and patterns. Plain squares and rectangles make sensible designs that link well with the architectural lines of a building. When laying them, be sure to start the pattern from a corner of the house or other obvious feature. Crazy paving, with its busy lines, looks best if sited some distance from the nearest building. The somewhat bold effect of hexagons, pentagons, and other multi-sided slabs can be softened and complemented by mature planting. Now available are small, interlocking paving blocks, ideal for drives, the patterns helping to enliven the appearance of large, uninteresting surfaces.

LAYING SLABS
There are three methods, depending on the use the surface is to be put to.

(1) Make a base of compacted hardcore (stones or pieces of broken bricks) and lay each slab on five 'spots' of 3:1 mortar (3 parts sand to 1 of cement). Adequate for most garden requirements.

(2) Bed the slabs on a continuous layer of mortar laid over a hardcore foundation. Ideal for drives and other areas subject to heavy use. NB: Drains or water pipes under such paving will be awkward to reach in an emergency.

(3) Spread a 50 mm (2 in) bed of raked sand over well-compacted ground. The slabs are simply bedded onto the sand. Rain can, however, undermine such a foundation.

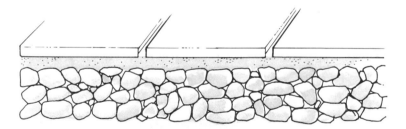

Precast slabs resting on five mortar spots over compacted hardcore

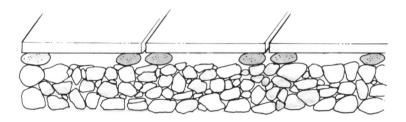

Precast slabs laid on layer of mortar over compacted hardcore

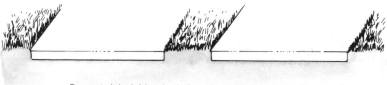

Precast slabs laid on bed of sand over compacted soil

NATURAL STONE PAVING Natural stone is a superb, but expensive paving material. Rectangular slabs, which are best for garden work, are often heavy enough to be laid on a simple bed of sand or, at most, on five spots of 3:1 mortar over compacted hardcore. Make sure that the paving pattern consists of a reasonable balance of larger and smaller stones and that the joints are staggered.

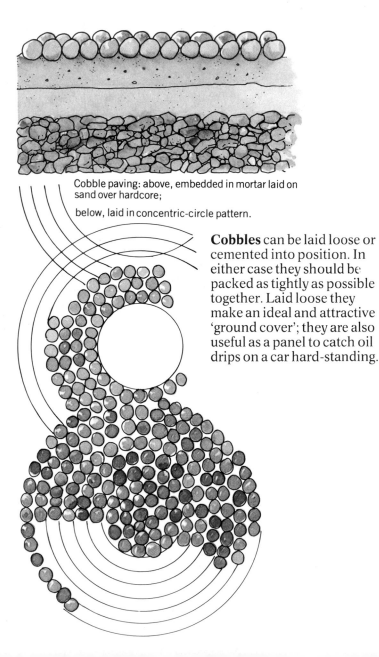

Cobble paving: above, embedded in mortar laid on sand over hardcore;

below, laid in concentric-circle pattern.

Cobbles can be laid loose or cemented into position. In either case they should be packed as tightly as possible together. Laid loose they make an ideal and attractive 'ground cover'; they are also useful as a panel to catch oil drips on a car hard-standing.

Stable pavers (below) are extremely hard and their architectural line makes them an excellent choice for use close to the house or an outbuilding.

BRICK PAVING

Traditionally, brick paving is laid on a dry bed of mortar over a suitably prepared base. More mortar is then brushed into the joints and the whole surface is carefully watered with a can fitted with a rose. For a slightly more durable result you can use a wet mortar mix and point the joints, but be careful to keep the surface of the bricks clean.

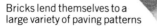

Bricks lend themselves to a large variety of paving patterns

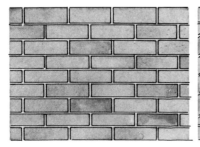

12 GRAVEL This is one of the most versatile and at the same time inexpensive materials for surfacing paths and drives.

Many people hesitate to use gravel for fear they will constantly be bringing it into the house on their shoes. In fact, this problem can largely be eliminated by selecting the optimum size of stones – about 20 mm (¾ in) in diameter is best – and by thorough preparation of the site; in particular, careful rolling at each stage is crucial.

First of all, prepare a base of hardcore not less than 150 mm (6 in) thick and thoroughly rolled or, better, rammed down. This should be topped with a 50 mm (2 in) layer of coarse gravel; then hoggin (a clay binder available at most builders' merchants) is spread to fill in all the cracks and rolled over the entire surface. Finally a layer of washed gravel between 25 and 40 mm (1-1½ in) thick is applied and rolled.

Edging is both visually important and practical in that it prevents the gravel from spreading. Use bricks on edge, laid end to end, and set into a concrete base.

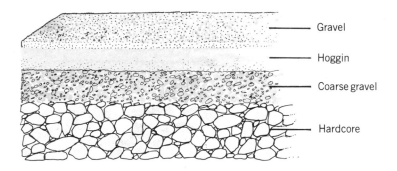

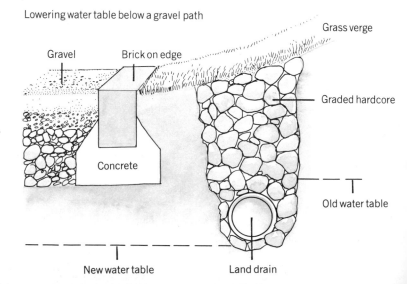

Lowering water table below a gravel path

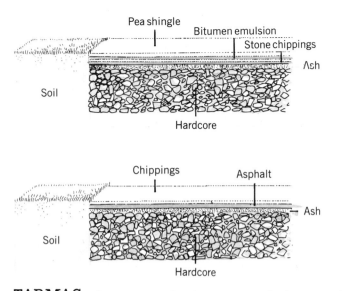

Pea shingle
Bitumen emulsion
Stone chippings
Ash
Soil
Hardcore

Chippings
Asphalt
Ash
Soil
Hardcore

TARMAC There are two basic tarmac surfacing materials available, asphalt and bitumen; the latter being the more suitable for drives. A base of hardcore or concrete should be prepared, the former vigorously rammed flat and covered with ash. **Bitumen** emulsion is laid using a watering can, covered with stone chippings, thoroughly rolled, and left for two weeks. A second coat of bitumen is then applied and covered with smaller stones, washed pea shingle being ideal.

Asphalt can be applied cold from bags and raked over the blinded hardcore base. Roll immediately and add a suitable top dressing. Bitumen and asphalt paths and drives must have a camber or a gradient to assist drainage.

A large, wide drive of bitumen or asphalt has a monotonous appearance. One way to add visual interest to your drive is to build up a pattern of **tarmac squares** separated by similar squares or walks of concrete slabs or bricks (below).

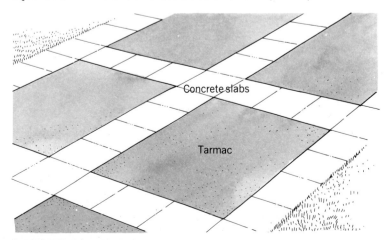

Concrete slabs

Tarmac

14 SLEEPERS AND WOOD BLOCKS Timber **railway sleepers** are ideal for paving, for raised beds, or even a sandpit (below), and need minimal foundations. When constructing a wall use a staggered bond. If you intend going above three courses, drill vertical holes through the sleepers, pass steel rods through each, and hammer them into the ground.

Tree-trunk slices on compacted soil make ideal paving for paths and informal sitting areas.

Old wood blocks formerly used to pave city streets are sometimes available from local councils. They can be used in much the same way as the tree-trunk slices, but lend themselves to a more formal architectural setting.

CONCRETE PAVING

Concrete can be laid in panels of almost any size or shape. Preparation of a suitable foundation is vital. Well-compacted hardcore 'blinded' with ash or a weak mix of concrete is the usual base. To maintain neat edges to the concrete, instal temporary **formwork** made of planks held in position by pegs. The top edges of the formwork should be at the planned level of the concrete surface. Check that the edge of each plank is horizontal (unless you require the concrete to slope) and the same height as the others by using a spirit level and a long, straight piece of board laid level across the drive.

After placing the concrete, use a **levelling board,** made from 150 x 50 mm (6 x 2 in) plank, to tamp the surface down.

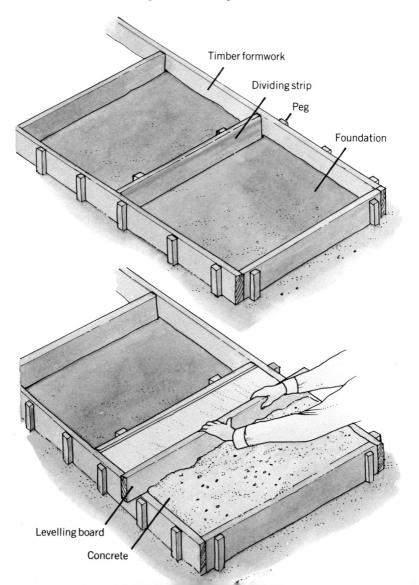

Timber formwork

Dividing strip

Peg

Foundation

Levelling board

Concrete

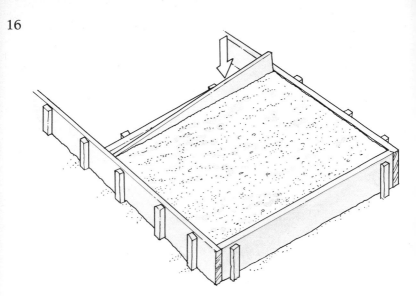

Expansion Joints Concrete may crack if it is laid as a continuous slab over too large an area. To overcome this problem lay it in 3 m (10 ft) maximum square or rectangular sections separated by expansion joints to allow each section to move independently. When laying a drive make sure that the joints are spaced at regular intervals. Part of the basic formwork must include **dividing strips** that are held in position by pegs. In front of each of these strips insert an expansion joint (above) – a thin softwood board of the same width and depth as the concrete (bricks or stonework can also be used). Once the concrete has been tamped down, the dividing strips can be removed (below), leaving the expansion joint to be sandwiched when the next panel is complete.

Concrete surface finishes: Brushed

Exposed aggregate

Wooden float

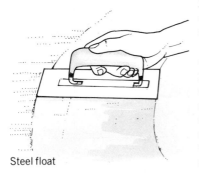

Steel float

Surface Finishes Once the
concrete has been thoroughly
tamped down, its surface can
be given a smooth, ribbed,
dimpled, or even marbled
finish. The effect of each of
the various finishes
mentioned below will vary
depending upon the length of
time the concrete has been
left before treatment begins. It
is a sensible idea to make
practice finishes on an
out-of-the-way portion of the
concrete before you work on
the entire surface. Many of
these finishes are not only
attractive in appearance but
help to make the surface less
slippery under foot. A brush
drawn over, rather than
pushed across, the surface
will produce a finely rippled
effect. Brushed aggregate can
look most attractive. This
involves leaving the surface
until it has nearly set. It is then
dampened from a watering
can and carefully brushed,
until the small stones and
aggregate in the cement mix
are exposed. A board,
somewhat lighter than
the tamping beam, can
be gently and carefully
worked to give a surface of
closely spaced ridges, ideal
for a sloping drive.
A wooden float gives a rough
finish, while its steel
counterpart smoothes out
every ripple.

The final job, once the drive
or path is complete, is to cover
it over while the concrete
dries. Damp sacks are ideal in
summer to prevent the
concrete from drying out too
quickly; dry sacking can be
used in winter to protect the
concrete against frost.

BRICK WALLS Brick boundary walls, internal-division walls, and raised beds form an integral part of many gardens.

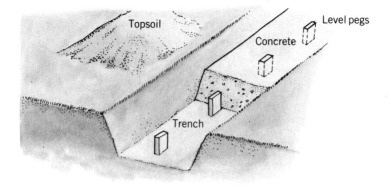

Foundations are essential. If the soil lacks firmness, dig a foundation trench 150 mm (6 in) deeper than your planned foundation concrete, and fill with well-compacted hardcore before concreting. The width of the foundation should be twice that of the finished wall. To establish levels, drive pegs into the trench bottom (above) to such a depth that the top of each peg represents the surface of the concrete foundation. After placing the concrete, level it and leave for a week before bricklaying.

Brick bonds are the patterns in which bricks are laid. If you are a beginner, use a simple Flemish bond (below), which uses 'closers' – bricks cut lengthwise in half – at the corners.

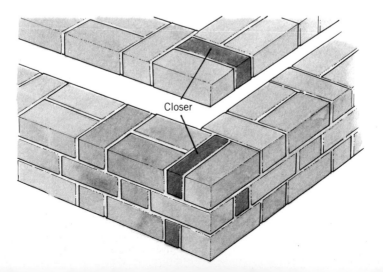

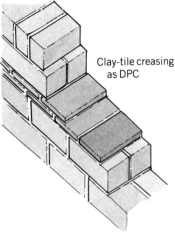

Engineering bricks (blue) used as DPC

Clay-tile creasing as DPC

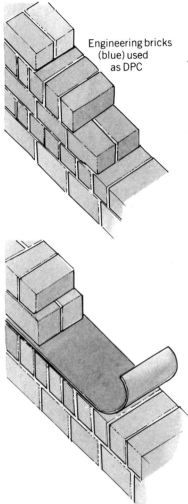

Damp-proof courses (DPCs) are an essential feature of every external wall; they prevent moisture from percolating into the wall from the ground. A layer of bituminous felt (left), the same width as the wall, should be incorporated between the second and third courses above the finished ground level.

Coping At the top of a wall coping does a similar moisture-excluding job to the damp-proof course at the base. Bricks on edge is a sensible choice, and you can also incorporate a 'creasing' of staggered clay tiles under the coping. Other coping materials include natural stone and precast concrete, as well as specialised zinc or copper strips.

Clay-tile coping: (left) correct style, with tiles flush with wall face

Clay-tile coping: (right) incorrect style — overhang traps rain water

20 ORNAMENTAL WALLS

There are so many shapes, sizes, and patterns of ornamental wall blocks available that it is often difficult to make a choice. As with most facets of design, the simple things usually work best.

An attractive wall can be built from **honeycomb brickwork** (above), in which a 75 mm (3 in) gap is left between each brick.

Landscape Bloc (below), a proprietary product, can be built up to form a wall, laid side by side to act as a retaining wall for a raised bed, or even double as table and chairs.

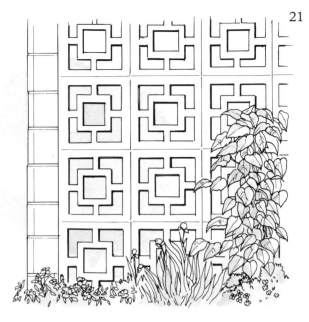

Various designs of **concrete blocks** are available. **Pierced screen wall block** (above) are typical and have been used widely in recent years. Other popular forms have simple **moulded faces** (below) that stand out in relief. **Flint-aggregate panels** (right) look attractive in the right environment. Use simple coping on all these walls.

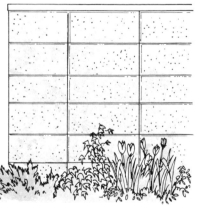

BARBECUE

Outdoor barbecue parties are becoming increasingly popular. If you are an enthusiast for eating outdoors, why not include a permanent barbecue in the layout of your patio or terrace. A purpose-built barbecue could be partly enclosed by walls to provide screening.

The barbecue shown has an adjustable cooking grid, the grill is available from hardware stores. Available sizes may determine the width of the cooking area. The worktop has a store beneath it for tools and supplies of charcoal.

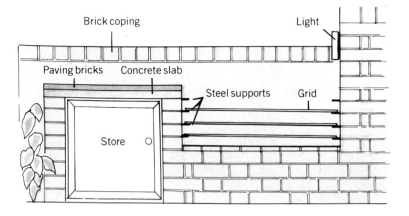

Construction The barbecue is built in brickwork using a straightforward Flemish bond. Remember that cut 'closer' bricks are used at the end and corners of the wall to adjust the bond. Suitable concrete foundations will be necessary and a simple brick-on-edge coping provides an unobtrusive finish for the top of the walls. As the brickwork rises in the cooking area, incorporate eight mild-steel supports (four at each side) to carry the charcoal and cooking grids. Below cooking level the barbecue is solid, the cavity formed by the walls being filled with rubble and hardcore. This is screeded with concrete, then paving bricks are laid as the finished surface. The floor of the **store** is similarly screeded, a timber shelf being fitted to battens screwed into the brickwork. The door is of simple ledge-and-brace construction. The roof of the store is constructed from a concrete slab, which is topped with more paving bricks.

Light fittings (see page 48) should be simple, unobtrusive, and well sited. In this example the cable could be laid under the adjoining paving and run up the back of the wall, where it would be screened by planting.

Obviously the exact design and overall shape of the barbecue, store, and seat will depend on the space at your disposal. There are, however, several general design points that are worth bearing in mind. Try to arrange that the shape of the barbecue fits in with the surrounding paving, so that (for instance) the joints between slabs line up with the ends of walls. If you are designing the patio and barbecue from scratch, you might like to consider paving at least part of the patio with the same kind of bricks as you are using to build the barbecue – and these, in turn, should match those (if any) used in the house walls, so lending harmony to the whole design.

REPOINTING BRICKWORK Pointing or repointing a wall provides it with protection against the weather. To remove old mortar, use a pointing chisel and club hammer, cutting back 15 mm (½ in) into the wall surface. Brush the wall to remove dust and chippings. Place a long board at the base of

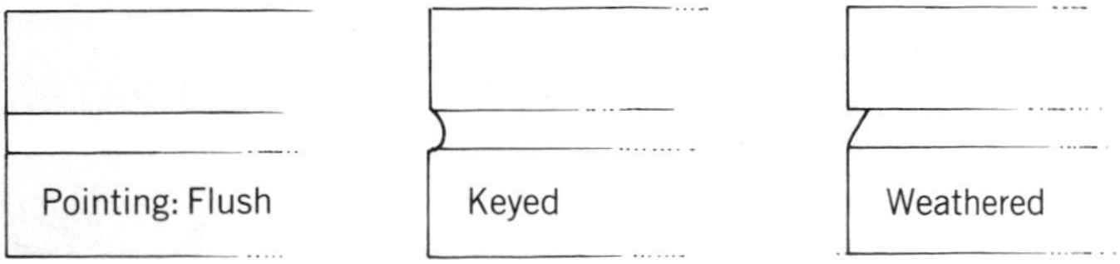

the wall to catch dropped mortar. A suitable mix uses 1 part cement, 6 parts soft sand, and 1 part plasticiser. Dampen the wall – approximately one square metre at a time – and fill the vertical joints first. Pointing can be flush, keyed, or weathered, but always match this with older existing work. Weathered pointing will need trimming off with a 'Frenchman' which can be made from an old knife. Bend 25 mm (1 in) of the tip at right angles and use this against a straight edge held just below the joints in the brickwork.

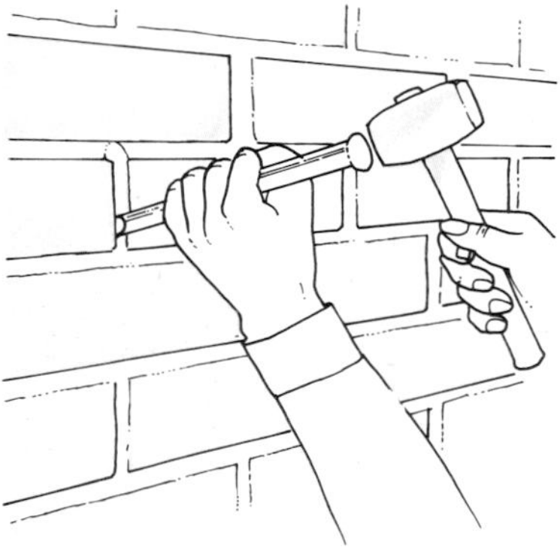

Repointing: Remove old mortar with pointing chisel and hammer.

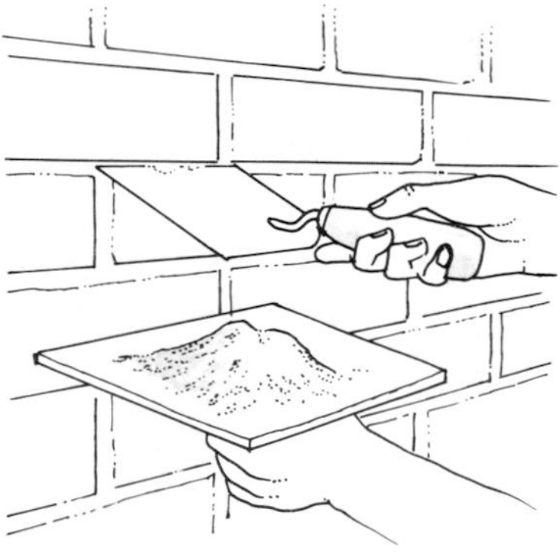

Apply fresh mortar, first to vertical joints, to dampened wall.

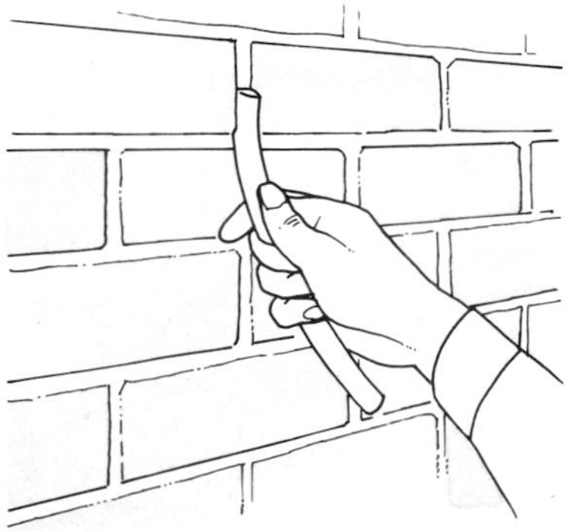

Keyed profile can be made with old pail handle or piece of rubber piping.

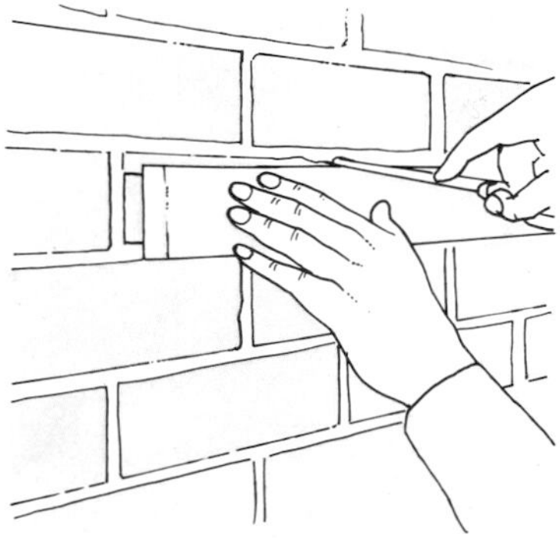

Weathered profile can be made with 'Frenchman' and straight-edge.

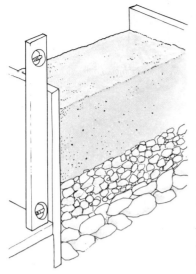

RAISED BEDS

A simple bed can be built from 900 x 600 mm (3 x 2 ft) precast concrete paving slabs. These are set in a trench 1.2 m (4 ft) wide and 300 mm (12 in) deep. Position the slabs upright, checking this with a spirit level, so that 600 mm (2 ft) shows above the surrounding paving. Fork over the bottom of the trench and place a layer of hardcore on the inside to keep the slabs vertical. Strips of polythene covering the joints on the inside will prevent excessive seepage during wet weather. When the walls are complete, line the bottom of the bed with a 150 mm (6 in) layer of broken stone or crocks, then fill with topsoil.

Base of concrete-slab raised bed is of compacted hardcore overlain with broken stone or crocks, with earth and topsoil filling. Check verticals often during construction.

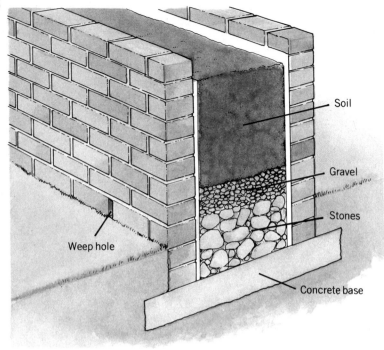

Soil

Gravel

Stones

Weep hole

Concrete base

DOUBLE WALL Useful in a paved area, a double wall (above) provides definition, enclosure, and partial division of the space. Like a raised bed it should be of a generous size so that the soil within it does not dry out too quickly. An ideal height is 450-600 mm (18-24 in) so that it can be used as a seat. Bricks, blocks, sleepers, and stone are all suitable materials.

DRY-STONE WALLS
These should be no higher than 1.5 m (5 ft) and built to a batter (wider at the bottom than at the top), and based on a firm stone or concrete foundation. Through-stones (those going the entire width of the wall) help to tie the work together. If possible, use local stone.

Coping stone

Through-stone

Foundation stone

STEPS

The ways in which you link changes of level can make or mar a garden, and it is desirable that purpose-built steps are made to seem an integral part of the overall composition. The choice of materials is vast, but dimensions are critical if the steps are to be easy on the eye and feet. As a general rule a 450 mm (18 in) tread (the distance from front to back of each step) with a 150 mm (6 in) riser is ideal for garden work. The depth of foundations will vary according to the site conditions and are similar to those for a brick wall.

If the steps serve a paved area, match the materials and ensure that the treads are so laid that no puddles form that could freeze in winter. Each tread should overhang the riser below it by 50 mm (2 in), so that an attractive shadow is cast below each step. If the ground is well compacted it may be possible simply to bed the bottom tread in mortar on the ground behind the riser, building each subsequent riser off the tread below. If the ground is soft the area beneath each step will need excavating and replacing with rammed hardcore; construction being carried out as before. If you are building a flight into or out from a paved area, you will need to construct retaining walls, again built off suitable foundations, on either side of the steps.

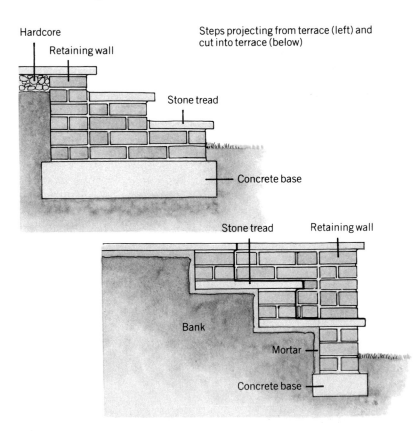

Hardcore
Retaining wall
Steps projecting from terrace (left) and cut into terrace (below)
Stone tread
Concrete base

Stone tread   Retaining wall
Bank
Mortar
Concrete base

Brick steps

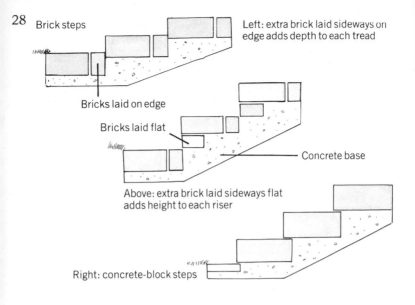

Left: extra brick laid sideways on edge adds depth to each tread

Bricks laid on edge

Bricks laid flat

Concrete base

Above: extra brick laid sideways flat adds height to each riser

Right: concrete-block steps

Unusual Step Designs Although steps are usually built to a rectangular layout, consider the possibility of using other shapes, sizes, and materials.

If there is ample space you could construct steps from a series of large overlapping circles or hexagons or various other shapes of concrete, grass, gravel, or tarmac, with plants both growing through and softening the outline. Cantilevered steps look splendid in the right situation, but you must ensure that construction is sound and that at least half of each step is bedded into the supporting wall.

Timber steps can look just right in informal gardens. Railway sleepers can be bedded into a bank in a staggered pattern; logs can be laid lengthways (in which case they will need to be kept in position by means of vertical stakes, as in the drawing) or shorter lengths can be driven in vertically; in the latter case, make sure that the logs are at least 125 mm (5 in) in diameter and their ends square and flush with each other.

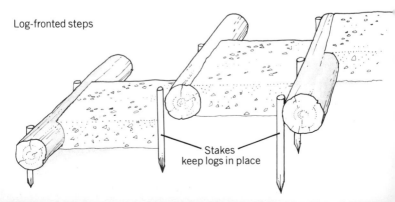

Log-fronted steps

Stakes keep logs in place

SINK GARDEN

Genuine stone sinks are expensive, but an artificial stone sink can be made by using an old porcelain sink as a base, the plug hole allowing excellent drainage. Clean and degrease the sink, then paint it with a suitable adhesive, such as Unibond. When this becomes tacky, artificial rock can be bonded to the surface of the sink. Make the 'rock' from a dryish mix of 1 part cement, 2½ parts sand, and 1½ parts peat. Apply it to the sink by hand (wear rubber gloves), building up layers approximately 15 mm (½ in) thick. Before the mix sets, go over its surface carefully with a stiff hand-brush in order to simulate the texture of real stone. Allow the sink to stand for several weeks and make sure you wash it well before planting.

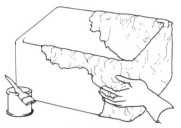

Applying mortar/peat mix to tacky sink surface

Creating rock-like surface texture with stiff brush

SLATE WATER FEATURE The basic components of this feature are a thick piece of slate (or millstone), a plastic water tank, a submersible pump, bricks, boulders, and cobbles, two lengths of corrugated plastic roofing, and sand and cement.

The tank is positioned on a 50 mm (2 in) bed of level sand; a weak mix of concrete is placed around the sides to give it stability. Two brick piers are built up to a point just below the tank's rim, and the pump is positioned between them. The slate is drilled to accept a 15 mm (½ in) diameter pipe, which is passed through it and connected to the pump. The open sides between the piers are closed with the plastic roofing, and the remaining area in the tank is filled with boulders and topped with loose cobbles. The tank is filled with water, and the pump circulates water through the slate and around the system.

PLANTING IN HALF BARRELS

The trouble with most plant containers is that they are too small, drying out quickly and becoming a real problem when you are away on holiday. Barrels make an ideal host for virtually all plants.

If the barrels are in one piece, saw them in half to make large tubs of equal size. Clean the tubs thoroughly, then bore three or four 15 mm (½ in) holes in the bottom. Paint a coat of non-toxic wood preservative on the inside, and spread a layer of broken crocks over the bottom before filling it with soil or compost. You can stain or paint the outside.

DISGUISING MANHOLE COVERS

A manhole is always a problem, invariably being in the wrong place in the garden. If it is in a paved area, rather than placing a tub over it, leave a gap around it and create a composition of boulders, loose cobbles, and low, spreading plants; all of these can be moved if you need access to the manhole. If you have a manhole in the middle of your lawn, make sure that the turf is slightly higher than the cover; the surrounding grass will soften its outline, making it virtually invisible but you will be able to mow the lawn right up to the edges.

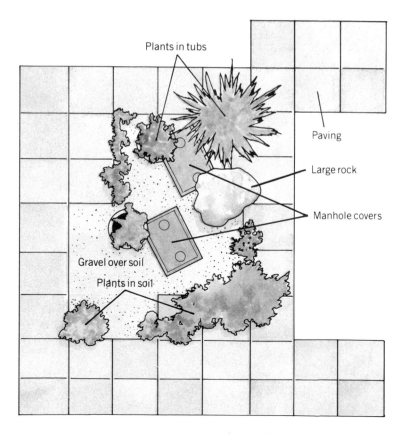

Plants in tubs

Paving

Large rock

Manhole covers

Gravel over soil

Plants in soil

32 WINDOW BOXES Cut

seven pieces of softwood to fit the dimensions of the window sill. For the sides, ends, and bottom use 25 mm (1 in) nominal timber; the 'feet' should be 50 mm (2 in) square, tapered to make the box horizontal on a sloping sill. Fasten the box securely to the sill. Use waterproof woodworking adhesive and screw all the joints with 40 mm (1½ in) brass screws.

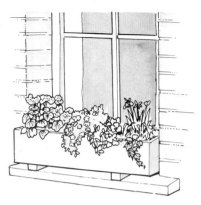

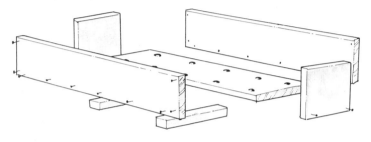

GARDEN FRAME This

consists of a box without a floor, having a glazed top sloping at about 12 degrees towards the front. Sensible dimensions are 1.5 m (5 ft) by 750 mm (30 in), the top being made of two or four panes divided by glazing bars. The ideal structural material is 20 mm (¾ in) exterior-grade plywood. Paint or stain the frame, and stand it on a base of dry-laid bricks.

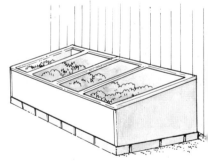

Sliding top
(end section)

Glazing bar
(detail)

GREENHOUSE TYPES

For the amateur gardener, greenhouses come in two basic types, timber or aluminium alloy. Timber, in the form of red cedar, is the traditional material and will blend well into almost every garden setting, but it does need maintenance and occasional treatment with preservative to prolong its life. Aluminium, on the other hand, is tough and durable and, although not as visually attractive as timber, needs less maintenance; it does, however, lose heat more readily than timber because metal is a better conductor of heat than wood.

Whichever type of greenhouse you have, check that gutters are kept clear, that the glass is clean (and immediately replaced if a pane breaks), and any overhanging branches are cut back so that they cast no shadows on the glass.

Some of the latest aluminium houses incorporate patent **double-glazing systems** which can bring a real saving on fuel bills and also retain the sun's heat longer if the house is not artificially heated.

Many manufacturers make the job of erection an easy one, with readymade plinths of concrete or metal needing minimal **foundations.** Quite a number of houses, however, will need a solid concrete base under the walls, and this can be laid over well-compacted and blinded hardcore in a suitable trench. When digging out the trench, set aside the topsoil for use in the greenhouse borders. If you are erecting a timber greenhouse, it is most important to ensure that a **damp-proof membrane** is laid at ground level. A suitable material for this is 1,000-gauge plastic sheeting, which you can buy at a builders' merchants.

SHADING

Even early in the year direct sunlight is strong enough to damage tender cuttings and seedlings and for this reason it is advisable to instal a simple form of shading in your greenhouse. Plastic mesh is ideal for this. The mesh can be attached to the ridge with cotton tape or a simple batten. Pass the net behind a length of curtain wire at eave height and let it fall to the staging or to ground level. A batten attached to the bottom of the mesh will act as a roller and will keep the shading vertical.

INSULATION

A simple insulation system using clear PVC sheeting as a form of double glazing considerably reduces heat loss. If you have a timber house, use drawing pins for fixing the sheet; specially made suction pads are available for aluminium houses. Use clear adhesive tape to join the sheets, and glaze the ventilators separately. Make sure, when fitting the sheet, that there is a small but definite gap between the sheeting and the glass – a minimum of 15 mm ($\frac{1}{2}$ in) but more if possible. Use the sheeting only when necessary, as it encourages condensation and reduces light intensity.

34 GREENHOUSE BENCHING

Once the greenhouse is erected you will need staging (benching). Apart from cost, the advantage of making your own is that you can have it at precisely the height that is best for you – and this can prevent you getting back-ache if you do a lot of greenhouse work. The drawing shows benching at the fairly typical height of 750 mm (30 in). In depth it should extend from the side wall to the line of the door. Runs should not be longer than 2 m (6½ ft) and the basic framework can be built from 50 x 50 mm (2 x 2 in) softwood. Joints can either be halving and rebates, or the timbers can be simply attached to each other with coach bolts and timber connectors. Diagonal bracing of the legs will increase the rigidity of the structure.

The slatted top uses 50 x 25 mm (2 x 1 in) slats, set 15 mm (½ in) apart, and can be neatly finished at the front and rear with 25 x 25 mm (1 x 1 in) battens.

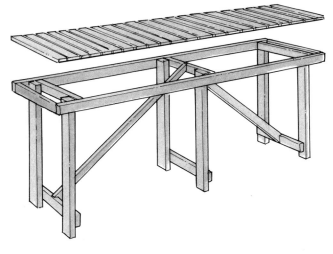

ROOF FELTING

Bitumen felt is a durable and inexpensive material for re-roofing a shed. Old material should first be carefully removed, and you should give particular attention to sites where old nail heads have been snapped off, leaving sharp points. Check all the boards underneath and replace any that are rotten or damaged, treating the new timber with a suitable preservative. The felt should be laid in wide sections, running along the length of the roof. In order to make the felt more workable cut the strips roughly to size and lay them flat for 24 hours before use. The first strips to be laid are those at eave level on each side; succeeding strips will overlap those below them; the last strip will be bisected by the roof-ridge. Roofing-felt adhesive will give added protection, and 15 mm ($\frac{1}{2}$ in) galvanised clout nails should be spaced at 50 mm (2 in) intervals. Fold edges under before nailing, and use a 350 mm (14 in) wide strip, fixed with adhesive, for the ridge.

FENCES Shelter is one of the most important requirements of any garden, and fences are probably the quickest and simplest way of providing this. The variety of fence heights and styles is enormous, however, and each serves a different purpose. A fence is essentially a physical barrier, but not all fences exclude a view. Some, for instance, simply mark the boundary of a property; at the other extreme a high, solid fence may be appropriate in a large garden, but in a small one it may cast unacceptably long shadows and induce a feeling of claustrophobia.

Chain link, wire netting, and **lattice** are all open fences in that they admit both views and draughts. Chain link, particularly the plastic coated variety, is extremely durable and forms a strong vandal-proof barrier. Wire netting looks much the same; it is cheaper but not nearly as strong. It makes a good temporary fence, however, and is of course ideal for animal enclosures. Lattice fences are made from timber lathes. They are not strong but are very suitable for internal divisions within the garden.

Closeboard, interwoven, and **interlock** fences are all solid and durable. They make a strong boundary for most gardens, confer privacy, and act as an unobtrusive background for plantings.

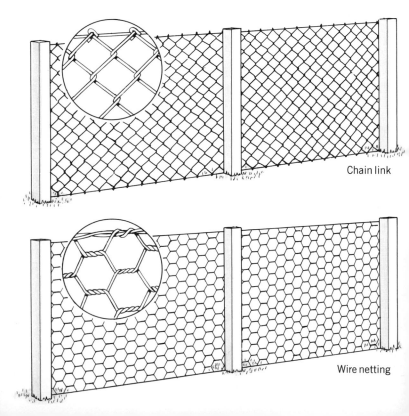

Chain link

Wire netting

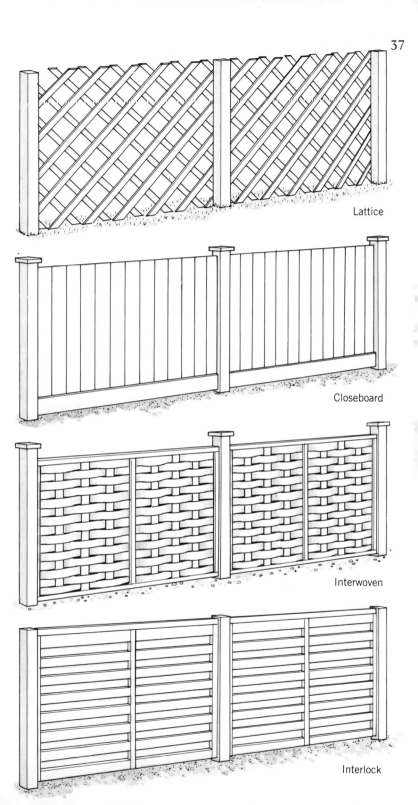

Lattice

Closeboard

Interwoven

Interlock

Wattle hurdle and **Norfolk reed** fences are cheap and often harmonise better with their surroundings than machine-made products. They do not last as long as sturdier types but make good screens for a young hedge.

Rustic fencing is made from untreated boughs and is most effectively used in an informal rural setting as a screen which may be softened by climbing plants.

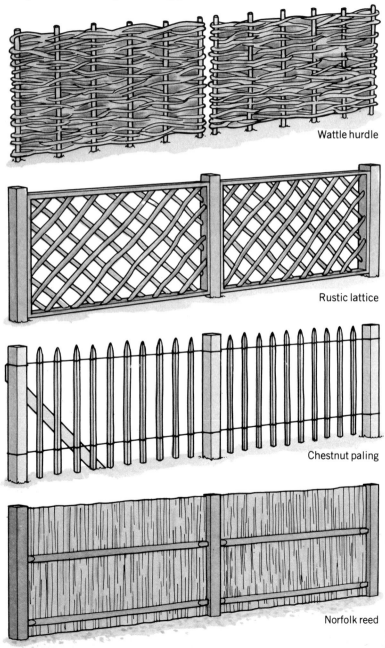

Wattle hurdle

Rustic lattice

Chestnut paling

Norfolk reed

Chestnut paling is also cheap but is rarely more than 1 m (3¼ ft) high. It makes a good temporary barrier with a rural flavour. **Picket fencing** has a crisp, front-garden feeling to it, while **post and chain** needs to be carefully used if it is not to look pretentious. **Post and rail** is ideal if one wishes to retain a view but needs to exclude livestock. **Ranch** fencing is perhaps over-used, but its architectural simpleity is attractive.

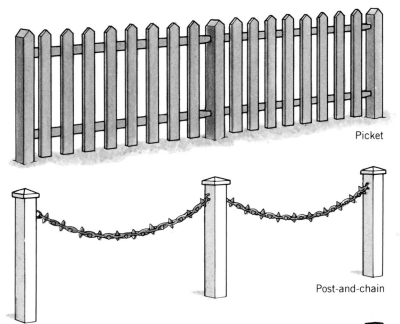

Picket

Post-and-chain

Post-and-rail

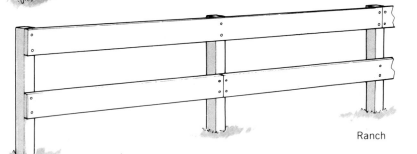

Ranch

FENCE POSTS These must be strong and really firm. You can hire a post-hole borer, which looks something like a giant corkscrew.

Each post must be sunk at least 600 mm (2 ft) in the ground. Dig the hole slightly deeper than this and fill the bottom with rammed hardcore to drain excess water away. Soil can be rammed around the post, but concrete provides a far more durable fixing. Before and during concreting (or earth ramming) check that the post is at the correct height and absolutely vertical; if necessary attach temporary supporting struts. The concrete should be brought just above ground level and chamfered off.

Post

Concrete with chamfered surface

Erecting the Fence Close-board fences have two or three arris rails, the latter being essential for a fence more than 1.5 m (5 ft) high. If the posts are without mortices, these will have to be cut. Concrete posts, which are more durable than wood, often have wedge-shaped mortices. If you use concrete posts they may have a slot at the bottom to accept a gravel board; if not, upright battens will need concreting in with the post so that the boards can be attached later.

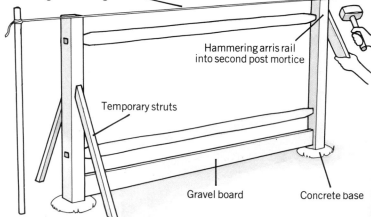

Line for height and straightness

Hammering arris rail into second post mortice

Temporary struts

Gravel board

Concrete base

Once the first post is in position and securely anchored with temporary struts, the arris rails can be fitted. A second person will be useful to hold the second post while you fit the rails, driving these well home with a club hammer and block of wood. If you are using timber posts, nail through to fix the arris rails to the first post, then check the second for vertical alignment and height, wedging it as necessary. The remainder of the run can now be completed in the same way. On concrete posts the gravel boards should be fitted at the same time as you fit the arris rails.

Fitting the Boards The final job with close-boarded fences is to fit the vertical boards. With a feather-edge type, start by placing the thicker edge of a board against a post, nailing it through the thickest part into the middle of the arris rails. Overlap by 15 mm (½ in) with the thicker part of the second board, again nailing through the thickest section. A spacer block will allow you to check the overlap required. Make sure that each board is absolutely vertical.

For a fence on a slope, the panels of vertical boards between the posts will have to be stepped. On a gentle slope it will look better if you step the fence only every two or three panels. The length of the post at each step will need to be greater than normal by the height of the step; and, similarly, the heights of the mortices on opposite sides of this post will differ by the size of the step.

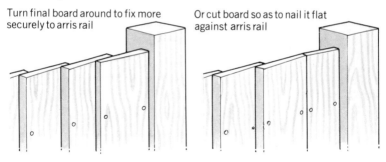

Turn final board around to fix more securely to arris rail

Or cut board so as to nail it flat against arris rail

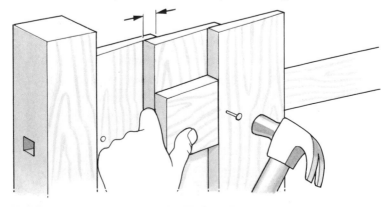

Cut small square of wood to act as spacer for fitting boards

42 REPAIRING FENCES A

well-maintained fence lasts a long time: check it every year at the end of the winter. Apply a non-toxic preservative every two years. Posts at ground level are particularly susceptible to rot; if it has not bitten too deep, rot may be arrested by clearing away the soil and allowing preservative to soak into the timber. If the damage is great (but the timber above ground is still sound – see 1), the

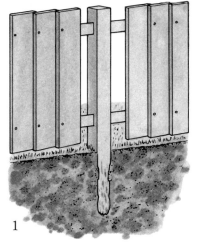

bottom of the post can be sawn off and a **concrete spur** substituted. This must be carefully positioned for height and verticality in a prepared hole, and the spur and the bottom of the retained section of timber post should overlap by at least 300 mm (12 in); the positions of bolt holes, which are built into the spur when it is made, are then marked on the post (see 2) and the latter drilled accordingly. Set the spur in concrete, bolt the post on, (washers with the bolt nuts), and fit temporary struts to prevent the spur moving while the concrete sets.

If an entire post on a close-boarded fence needs to be replaced, the boards on either side of the post must be removed (see 3). Cut through the arris rails close to the post, and then lift the latter out of the ground. The new post must be set at the same height as the old and should preferably be sunk in concrete. The arris rails can be repaired by attaching additional lengths by means of scarf joints.

FEDGES

A fedge is a combined fence and hedge. Fedges make ideal screens and divisions within a garden. For a screen up to 2 m (6½ft) high, sink 75 mm (3 in) square posts 600 mm (2 ft) in the ground and attach heavy-duty plastic mesh to both sides with galvanised staples. For a lower fedge architectural shapes can be built up using bent steel reinforcing rod. Use a vice for this; a plywood template will enable you to produce rods of a regular shape and size. The rod ends can be slotted into lengths of scaffold pole set in the ground. Connect the hoops with plastic net, tied with rot-proof string.

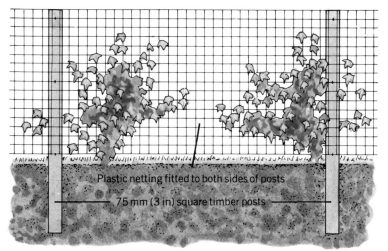

Plastic netting fitted to both sides of posts

75 mm (3 in) square timber posts

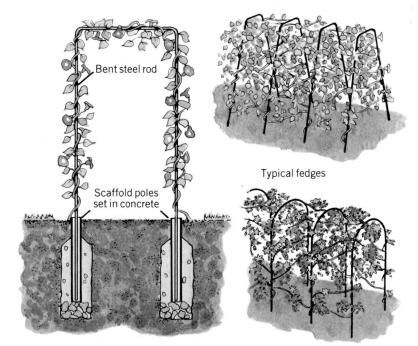

Bent steel rod

Scaffold poles set in concrete

Typical fedges

GATE TYPES

Gates are important: they can make or mar the appearance of the boundary of a property, and they can be used to reflect the theme or character of the garden to which they provide access.

The key word when selecting a gate is harmony – harmony with both the nature and the materials of neighbouring objects in the garden. For instance, the tracery of a fancy wrought-iron gate is bound to appear incongruous if it is set into a traditional dry-stone wall. A sense of scale is also important; a massive five-bar gate makes an inappropriate entrance to a small cottage garden; and if you are making your own gate try to ensure that it respects the line of the wall, hedge, or fence into which it is set.

Gates should always open inwards rather than outwards, especially if they give directly onto a path or road. It is often possible to combine pedestrian and vehicle gates, thus saving the expense of making two breaks in a boundary.

GATE POSTS

Five-bar gates make an impressive entrance to a wide drive, but their weight means that the **hanging post** will have to be substantial. If the gate is set into a wall, piers will be more suitable than timber or concrete posts, the hinge pins on which the gate will hang being built into the brickwork at the appropriate heights. It is sensible to select gate fittings before erecting posts or piers, as these will determine the spacing of the latter.

Oak and Spanish chestnut are the best hardwoods for timber posts, and these should be treated with preservative rather than painted. Softwood posts should be pressure-treated with preservative, but can subsequently be painted. The hanging post should measure at least 250 mm (10 in) square in section and must be sunk at least 1 m (3¼ ft) in the ground. As with fence posts, the hole should be dug slightly deeper than this, the bottom filled with well-compacted hardcore, and the post set in concrete, temporary struts being installed to make sure the post does not drop out of true.

An interval of at least two weeks must elapse before the gate is hung. Hanging a heavy gate is a two-man job. Double-strap and hook hinges are most suitable, and the straps should be fitted to the hanging stile, or heel, of the gate first, with the larger strap at the top. The gate should then be offered up and supported on several lengths of timber, so that the position of the straps in relation to the hooks can be marked. Drill the post and fit the bolt, using suitable washers; alternatively, you can use traditional spiked hooks that are driven into the post. The gate can now be lifted onto the hooks, which should be lightly greased. A catch is finally fitted to the closing style or head of the gate and its post. The latter, incidentally, need not be as massive as the hanging post; a 150 to 200 mm (6 to 8 in) square section should be adequate.

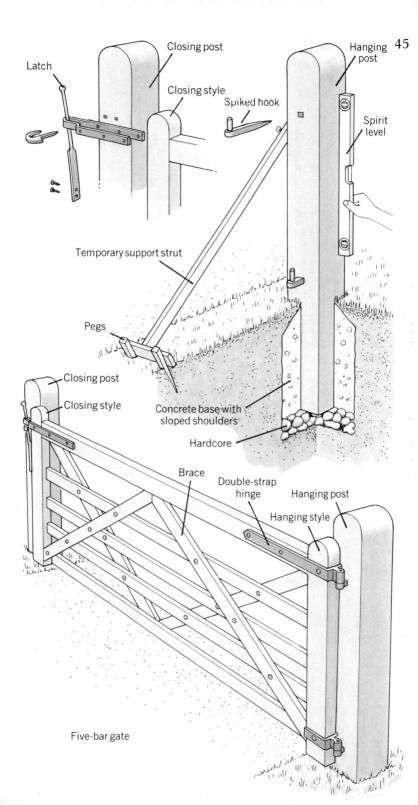

Latch

Closing post

Closing style

Spiked hook

Hanging post

Spirit level

Temporary support strut

Pegs

Concrete base with sloped shoulders

Hardcore

Closing post

Closing style

Brace

Double-strap hinge

Hanging post

Hanging style

Five-bar gate

GATE PIERS Brick piers are most suitable supports if a gate is to be set into a wall. For a simple pedestrian gate a 340 mm (13½ in) square brickwork pier is adequate; for heavier gates 450 mm (18 in) square or larger piers will be necessary.

Foundations must go 450 mm (18 in) below ground level and extend 150 mm (6 in) all round the base of the pier. To ensure the courses rise evenly, use a straight edge and spirit level extending between the piers. Fishtail hinges and a latch can be built into the piers at the appropriate height.

If you want to hang a gate to an existing house wall you will need first to fix a timber post to the building. This can be done with screw bolts which are cemented into the wall. Hinges can then be fitted to the post.

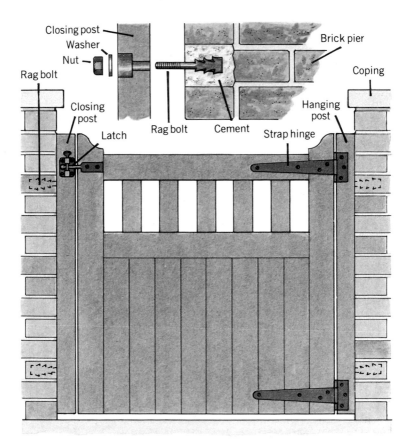

Troubles with gates usually involve **sagging** or **binding**. Sagging is usually due to inward movement of the hanging post, which must be reset in fresh concrete. It may also be due to distortion of the hinges which will then need to be fixed with longer screws or replaced. Binding is usually a product of sagging; but also check that the latch post is still vertical.

ELECTRICITY

The intelligent use of electricity can transform a garden, whether it be for lighting, powering above-ground or submersible pool pumps, or operating air-heating, soil-heating, propagation, and other greenhouse systems.

As far as **lighting** is concerned, the results can be both subtle and spectacular: a statue can be spotlighted, or the delicate tracery of foliage gently illuminated; darkness and shadow add a fascinating dimension to your outside room, while steps and paths will need to be clearly visible. Drives and garages are key points also, and one of the most effective deterrents to burglars are one or two well-sited spotlights.

As with most aspects of design, you will create the best effects if you keep the lighting simple and do not overdo things: a surfeit of lights will produce either over-complicated effects or a dully uniform illumination. Be selective with colour: white and blue are often the most effective, whereas some other shades turn foliage a sickly hue.

There is an enormous choice of fittings, but try to keep to a particular theme that relates to the character of your house and garden. Coachlights look ridiculous on a modern façade, as do lamp posts in a small garden. There are many especially fine modern fittings available that blend into virtually any setting, so shop around and choose what is right for you. For a pool a variety of fittings is available, including bottom-mounted, floating, and even automatically rotating lights. Here, too, simplicity pays; it is best to start with a modest display and, if you want to, build up from there.

It is a good idea, if you intend to go in for electrical DIY garden projects, to assemble a basic tool kit and keep it handy for when you need to carry out routine repair work. Among the more important items are a pair of pliers with insulated handles; an electrician's screwdriver; a wire-stripper of the type that can be adjusted to remove insulation on various thicknesses of cable without damaging the wire; a sharp knife; and a reliable battery torch.

SAFETY FIRST! Much effort has gone into making the use of electricity in the garden safe. Most lighting and pools systems are nowadays worked off a transformer which reduces power to 12 volts. If you are considering using mains voltage in the garden or greenhouse, there are a number of pre-wired sealed-lamp systems available – but you are strongly advised to leave their installation to a qualified electrician. Whatever system you decide to use, you will need to operate it from a separate fuse in your fuse box.

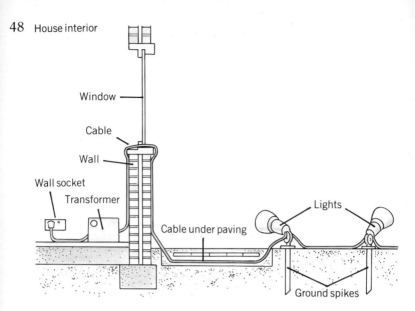

LIGHT FITTINGS
Mains voltage in the garden is the province of the qualified electrician. But you can certainly instal the outdoor part of the 12-volt systems that serve both lights and pool equipment. Outside waterproof sockets, single or multiple, need a separate 15-amp fuse in your fuse box, and this must be installed by the Electricity Board. All exterior materials must be weatherproof and the lights sealed. The lighting system will consist of a transformer that must be housed under cover and will take up to six lights. The lights themselves are fitted with ground spikes. Wiring up is by one of two systems: one involves placing the cable against a lightholder and screwing a special cover in place, forcing the cable wire against metal prongs on the lightholder; the other uses terminals within the lamp. The cable need not be buried.

POOL LIGHTS
The lights, usually available in pairs, are watertight, so can be weighted down to the bottom. The cable is taken back to a suitably positioned 12-volt transformer.

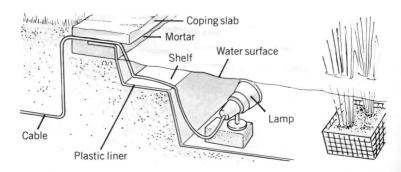

ELECTRICAL HEATING

In the greenhouse electrical heaters do much to extend the growing season of many crops, and there are many systems available.

You can heat propagators and frames (see drawings) and you can also use electricity to operate irrigation and mist systems and control ventilators and shading.

Frames can be heated in two ways, either by wires attached above soil level to the inside walls of the frame, or by cables buried in the ground.

Soil-heating aids propagation, while air warming is suitable for over-wintering tender plants. For propagation lay the cables on a 50 mm (2 in) bed of coarse sand and cover them with a further 50 mm (2 in) of sand.

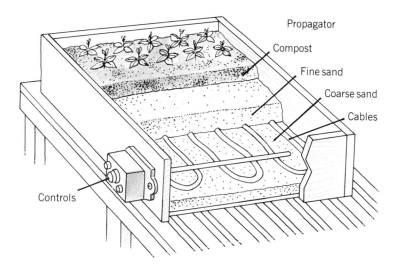

Propagator
Compost
Fine sand
Coarse sand
Cables
Controls

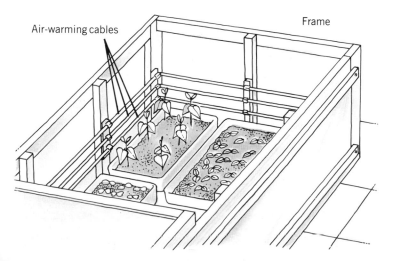

Air-warming cables
Frame

LARGE GLOBES These
simple fittings are essentially
updated coachlamps, but they
are far more attractive than
the latter in a contemporary
setting. Their unobtrusive
shape makes them ideal for
both formal and informal
situations; the globes can be
frosted or clear.

FLUORESCENT TUBE
This type of light is pure
sculpture and can be installed
singly or in groups. Various
lengths and shapes of
fluorescent fittings are
available. Siting is important:
these are essentially feature
lights for a formal position, so
make sure that the group
balances with the architecture
around it. Tube lights such as
these, incidentally, have a
much longer life than the
conventional tungsten bulbs,
and they are also cheaper to
run than tungsten bulbs of the
same wattage.

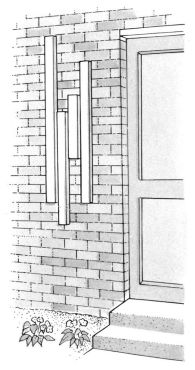

MUSHROOMS Lighting
manufacturers are now
producing an exciting variety
of organic shapes. Typical are
these 'mushrooms' that might
have sprouted from the lawn
overnight and are ideal for
illuminating shallow steps or
plantings. They look best if
sited in small clusters.

MORE MUSHROOMS

These larger mushrooms have been available for some time. They are ideal for siting in a border as they cast light downwards rather than dispersing it upwards. One or two carefully positioned will be more effective (and cheaper!) than several in a group.

BOLLARDS

These lights have a slightly 'municipal' feeling about them and are best employed for the front approach to the house, illuminating a drive or path. You will, of course, find it easier to set them in a planted area beside a hard surface rather than cutting slabs or other paving to fit around them.

ANTI-VANDAL LAMPS

Renewing the larger light fittings can be expensive, and for the front of the property it is worth installing lights that can stand up to occasional rough treatment. If they look practical rather than pretentious they are less likely to tempt vandals; for maximum security they should be fixed into solid concrete or brick bases.

GARDEN POOLS Water can be delightful in a garden, its sight and sound being both refreshing and relaxing especially, perhaps, in an urban situation. Unfortunately, garden pools are often sited with too little regard for their immediate surroundings and are ill-conceived in size, shape, and depth. As a general rule, the more open the aspect the better: few aquatic plants thrive in shade, and fish dislike water that has become polluted with leaves and other vegetation; sunshine is essential for healthy plants and fish.

The shape and size of a pool will, of course, depend largely on the site chosen. Water features sited close to the house demand architectural treatment – that is, a certain formality and a simple shape. For those in the farther reaches of the garden, informal free-flowing shapes will be more in keeping. It is worth remembering that you will rarely be looking at the pool from directly above; what may seem an attractive combination of curves on the drawing board may become a rather fussy scheme in reality. The most successful garden pools usually consist of a simple, unbroken stretch of water in which fish can flourish, where an uncomplicated fountain can play, and where you can obtain the maximum reflections. For all these purposes generous rectangular, circular, or oval shapes are probably the most effective.

If you have a change of level in a garden you might consider constructing a system of formal or informal **split-level pools,** where the water (circulated by a pump) spills from one level to the next in a series of waterfalls (see also page 62).

POOL TYPES Once you have decided on a suitable pool shape, there are two other important decisions to take: first, the profile of the pool; and second, the material from which the pool is to be constructed. The profile, or cross-section, has a considerable bearing on the ability of plants or fish to flourish in the pool. A normal garden pond needs to be no deeper than 600 mm (2 ft) and most of the floor should be at this sort of depth. Marginal plants should be set at a higher level, however, so you will need to build a shelf, about 200 mm (8 in) below the water surface and about 200 mm wide, which can go part or all of the way around the margin of the pond.

Until a few years ago, **concrete** was the only constructional material available for garden pools, but its tendency to crack under ice pressure or ground movement has led to a decline in its popularity. Plastic-based materials of various types are now more commonly used; they lend themselves to more complex shapes, especially curves, and require less hard work.

Glass-fibre pools are relatively expensive but, being pre-formed, are easy to instal. The drawback is that they are not always large enough to support a balanced environment. **Vacuum-formed** pools are cheaper and lighter than glass-fibre, but they too are available mainly in rather modest sizes.

Flexible plastic liners are available in rectangular sheets. If you are planning a free-form pool, remember that the more complicated its design the more wastage of liner will be involved. **Polythene liner** is cheap but fragile. It does not stretch and cannot be patched if it is holed. Apart from its possible use in a temporary pond, it is not recommended. **Laminated PVC** looks like polythene, but is tougher, is able to stretch, and lasts about 20 years. It is ideal for most pools. **Butyl liners** are the toughest of all, but are also the most expensive; they are ideal for large ponds or lakes.

Pool profiles

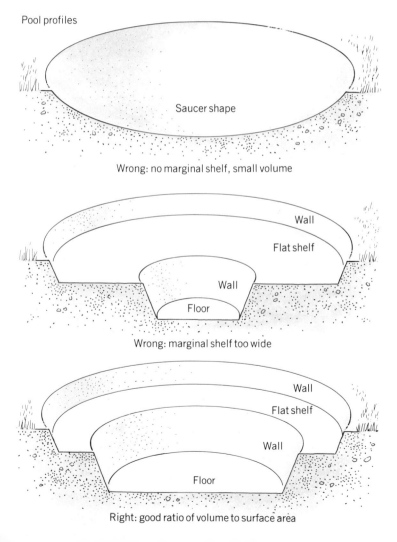

Wrong: no marginal shelf, small volume

Wrong: marginal shelf too wide

Right: good ratio of volume to surface area

PLASTIC-LINED POOL To calculate the size of a plastic pool liner, work out the maximum width and length of the pool and add twice the maximum depth to both these measurements; this will give you the overall size of the liner sheet. The ground around the pool must be level because the water surface should be equidistant from the coping at all points. Where the coping adjoins grass make sure that it is set just below the latter. Mark out the whole area of the pool and coping, swinging a line from a radius point to obtain curves. After turf has been lifted and stacked, mark out the shape of the pool itself and dig the entire area out to a depth of 200 mm (8 in) with the sides angled at 20 degrees from the vertical. Mark out the marginal shelves, then dig out the remainder of the pool to a depth of 600 mm (2 ft). In order to check the angles of the sides

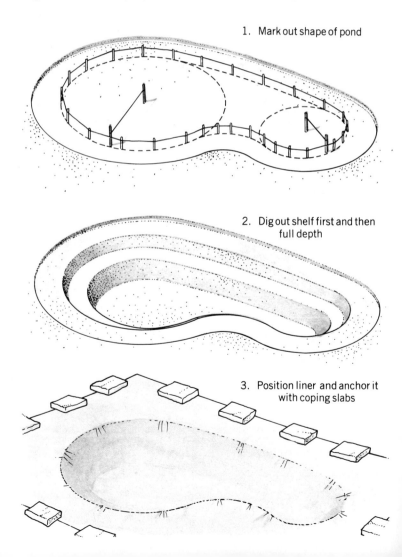

1. Mark out shape of pond

2. Dig out shelf first and then full depth

3. Position liner and anchor it with coping slabs

and the height and widths of shelves use a simple plywood or hardboard template.

Make sure that there are no sharp stones in the sides or bottom of the excavation, and then cover the bottom, shelves, and walls with about 15 mm (½ in) of damp, soft sand. Place the liner over the pool area and weight it down around the edges with bricks or loosely laid slabs. Water can now be run into the pool, stretching the plastic and gently moulding it to the exact shape of the excavation. When the pool is full, trim the liner to size, leaving a 225 mm (9 in) 'collar' around the edge of the pool. Cut the plastic where it is wrinkled at curves or corners in order to lay it flat, and finally lay the coping slabs on a 1:4 mortar mix, making sure each slab overhangs the water by about 50 mm (2 in).

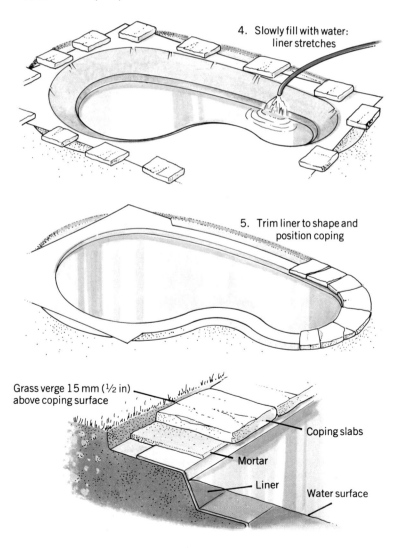

4. Slowly fill with water: liner stretches

5. Trim liner to shape and position coping

Grass verge 15 mm (½ in) above coping surface

Coping slabs

Mortar

Liner

Water surface

56 CONCRETE POOL

If you want to construct a concrete pool, keep the shape simple, preferably rectangular. This will make the job of fitting timber shuttering far easier. When determining the depth and area of the pool, bear in mind that you will have to excavate an area large enough to take a 150 mm (6 in) thick hardcore foundation and that the walls will need to be 125 mm (5 in) thick; the latter must slope at about 20 degrees from the vertical.

The **hardcore** must be thoroughly compacted and 'blinded' with a layer of sand. Chicken wire should be laid over the sand and up the sides of the excavation to act as reinforcement. Now place the concrete base, making sure the ingredients of 3 parts coarse aggregate, 2 parts sand, and 1 part cement are well mixed; a waterproofing additive (available from builders' merchants) should also be incorporated into the mix. The concrete must be worked through the netting.

Hardboard or plywood **shuttering** for the sides should be installed immediately you have completed the base. It is crucially important that the base and sides are able to set at exactly the same time, otherwise you are very likely to experience problems of leakage at the points where they meet. On the other hand it is essential that neither the shuttering nor the framework that supports it is allowed to rest its weight on the still-wet base. For this reason it is best to incorporate into the framework a series of extensions (as shown in the illustration) so that the full weight of both the framework and shuttering rests on the ground on either side of the pool. The object is to allow the bottom of the shuttering to be suspended to within about 6 mm (¼ in) or less of the pool base. To achieve this you can make fine adjustments to the depth of the shuttering by inserting offcuts or battens under the frame extensions. The same concrete mix is used for the sides as for the base, and the shuttering must be retained until the shell has set – it usually takes about 14 days. Then completely fill the pool with water to help the concrete to cure. After two days, remove the water.

A 25 mm (1 in) **rendering** will need to be applied to the walls, consisting of 3 parts sharp sand to 1 part cement, plus a waterproofing compound. The **coping** can be laid on a mortar mix, and should overhang the pool by 50 mm (2 in).

The pool cannot be stocked immediately, as free lime from the concrete will percolate into the water. The best and cheapest solution to the problem is to fill the pool and let it stand for two weeks, emptying it at the end of that time. Repeat this operation three times to ensure safety. Alternatively, you can paint the concrete surface with two or three coats of a proprietary sealant.

If you have 'inherited' a concrete pool through house purchase and find that it leaks persistently, the best thing to do is to drain and clean it, and then line it with a plastic liner, as described already.

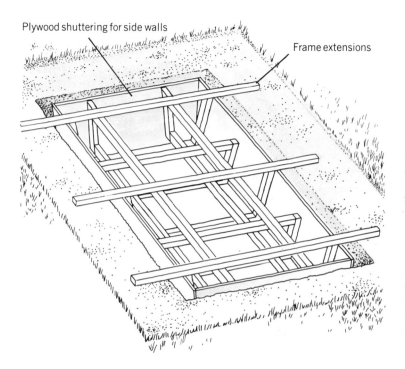

Plywood shuttering for side walls

Frame extensions

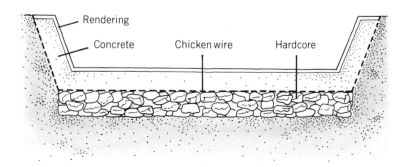

Rendering

Concrete

Chicken wire

Hardcore

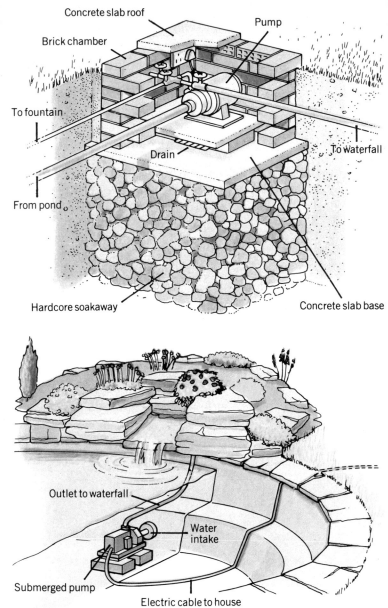

Concrete slab roof

Brick chamber

Pump

To fountain

To waterfall

Drain

From pond

Hardcore soakaway

Concrete slab base

Outlet to waterfall

Water intake

Submerged pump

Electric cable to house

WATER PUMPS
Moving water is not essential for healthy pond life, but it does considerably increase a pond's interest as a focal point of the garden. If the water flow is large use a **surface pump.** This must be placed in a brick chamber with drainage to a soakaway. Water is taken from the pond via a strainer and delivered to the outlets through gate valves. If the pool is of modest size, with a single fountain or small fall (but not both), use a **submersible pump,** placed just clear of the pool bottom.

WATERING SYSTEMS

Hoses attached to the kitchen-sink tap are a nuisance and impractical. It is far better to fit an **outside tap** that can service the garden separately. Before doing this, check with your area Water Authority: you may have to pay a slightly higher water rate for using non-hand-held appliances.

The tap should be taken off the **rising main** in 15 mm (½ in) copper tube, fitting a **stopcock** to isolate the line in winter. Pass the tube through the house wall and let it drop down to a **wall-plate elbow.** Fit a tap with a special hose bib. From the tap a hose can be run down the garden. There are two basic coupling systems available for a wide range of accessories. Fittings either **screw** together to form watertight joints, or they have a **snap action** that makes connection even easier.

A typical system might use a 'Y' piece from the main hose line. One arm of the Y might go to the vegetable garden, where a hand-held nozzle can deliver water ranging from a fine mist to a gushing stream; the other branch might go to an oscillating or pulsating sprinkler, set up in another part of the garden.

If you are running a pipe underground – for instance, to a greenhouse some distance from the mains supply – use alkathene pipe, burying it deep to avoid it being fouled later by garden tools. Make sure that any exposed tubing or standpipes are properly **lagged,** and always fit a stop cock to isolate the system in case your pipes ice up.

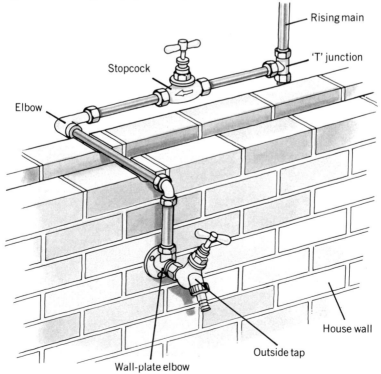

Rising main

'T' junction

Stopcock

Elbow

House wall

Outside tap

Wall-plate elbow

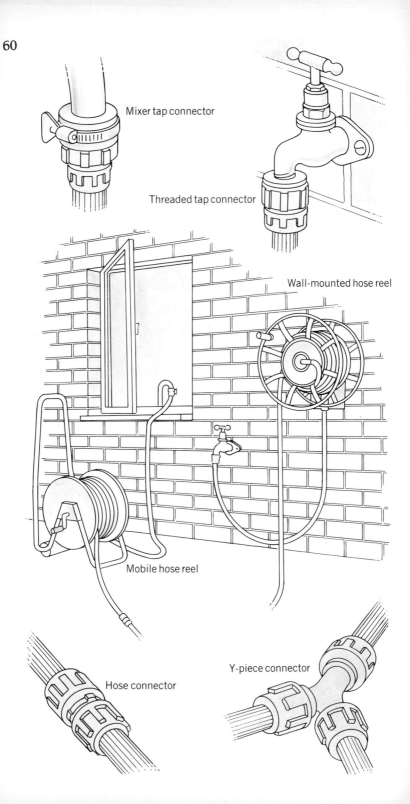

Mixer tap connector

Threaded tap connector

Wall-mounted hose reel

Mobile hose reel

Hose connector

Y-piece connector

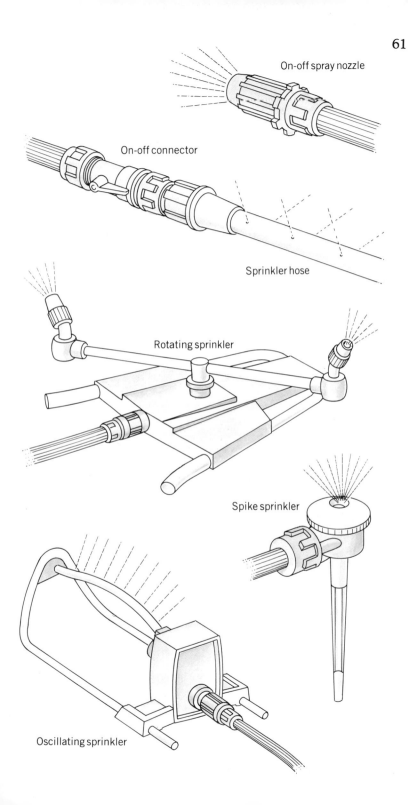

On-off spray nozzle

On-off connector

Sprinkler hose

Rotating sprinkler

Spike sprinkler

Oscillating sprinkler

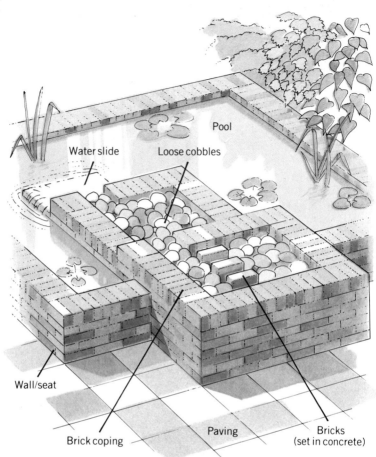

Pool

Water slide   Loose cobbles

Wall/seat

Brick coping   Paving   Bricks
                                      (set in concrete)

SPECIAL WATER FEATURE Water close to a building
or in an architectural setting needs careful handling if it is not
to clash with its surroundings. Raised pools can double as
occasional seats and are safer than water at ground level if you
have toddlers in the garden. Even more interest can be created
if you have split-level pools. The pool shown here has three
levels, and water is circulated through the system by a
submersible pump. The upper levels are simple **concrete slides**
set in a frame of 225 mm (9 in) brickwork. Water flows from an
outlet pipe within the top level through a bed of loose **cobble
stones.** The stream slides down to an intermediate level, and
finally drops to the pool.
    The effectiveness of this feature lies in its simplicity and its
attention to detail. The cobbles should be piled deeply, with no
concrete visible between them. The brick-on-edge **coping**
should overhang the water, throwing a soft shadow, while the
water slide to the bottom pool could be a single piece of **marble**
or even **plate glass.**

WATERCRESS GARDEN

Watercress is an extremely useful salad crop and can be grown quite easily in the garden. Running water is not essential to the plant, but a constant supply of water, preferably by means of a hose, is important. The cress needs shady conditions and plenty of organic material. Dig out a trench 600 mm (2 ft) wide and a spade deep and fill the bottom with a 150 mm (6 in) layer of well-rotted vegetable compost. Backfill the trench with the excavated topsoil to 100 mm (4 in) below the ground on either side.

Germinate the seeds in early April at a temperature of 13°C (55°F) in the greenhouse or propagator, harden off in a cold frame, and plant them outside about the first week in June. Make sure the trench is really damp when the plants are set out, and water them at least once a week by letting water run into the end of the trench.

Weekly watering

Topsoil

Compost

PROTECTING TREES Some trees, particularly conifers, are not easy to move, and when they have been transplanted they need protection from the wind. If you are moving a tree within the garden, give it a good watering several days beforehand and also spray the foliage with an anti-dessicant then and after transplanting to prevent excessive drying out. Dig out the new planting hole, making sure it is big enough to accommodate the full spread and depth of the roots. Position the tree carefully in the hole, and make certain it is upright. Thoroughly firm the soil around the base of the tree.

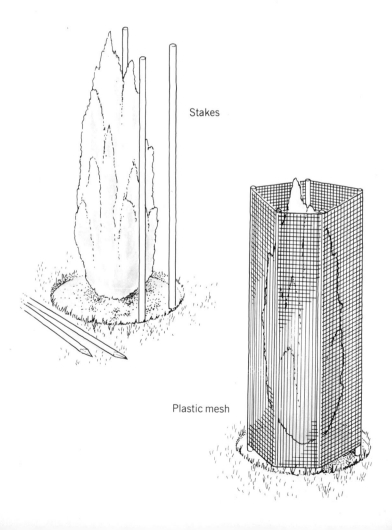

Stakes

Plastic mesh

STAKING TREES

All tall plants and particularly heavy or semi-mature trees need to be securely staked to prevent them rocking and to encourage the root system to develop as quickly as possible. There are two basic systems. The first of these uses three 75 mm (3 in) section (round or square) stakes, which must have been treated beforehand with preservative. Dig a pit of the required size, position the main stake that will support the tree, and drive it at least 600 mm (2 ft) into the ground. The stake should be on the windward side of the tree. Align two more stakes on either side of the first, fit a bracing strut, and nail this securely in position. Secure the stem to the middle stake with two plastic tree-ties. For **very heavy trees** three guy wires should be used, attached to wooden or metal stakes. The wires are passed through heavy-duty plastic hose pipes and looped around sturdy lower branches.

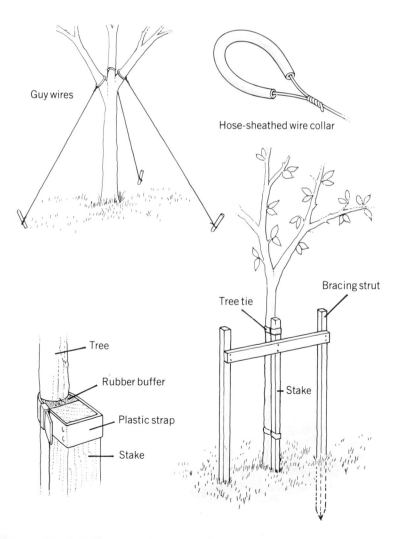

Guy wires

Hose-sheathed wire collar

Tree tie

Bracing strut

Tree

Rubber buffer

Plastic strap

Stake

Stake

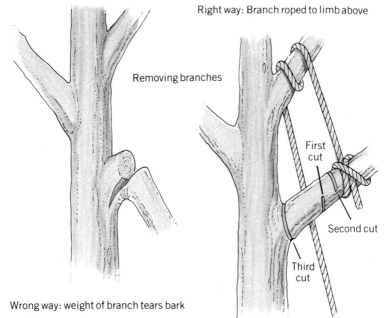

Right way: Branch roped to limb above

Removing branches

First cut

Second cut

Third cut

Wrong way: weight of branch tears bark

TREE FELLING
Felling a large tree, particularly a big elm that has been dead for some time, is strictly a job for professionals: the damage that could be caused by several tons of timber falling in the wrong direction does not bear thinking about.

Small trees can be simply felled, however, and there is no need to leave the routine job of removing dead limbs to the tree-surgeon. **Safety** is the prime consideration, both for yourself and for surrounding property. First, make sure there is sufficient room for the timber to fall, and remember that branches will extend farther than you think. If the trunk is substantial, a chain saw can be hired, but for most trees of reasonable size a **bow saw** is adequate. The first cut will be on the side of the direction of fall; it will be relatively shallow and can be enlarged into a wedge shape. The second cut will be on the opposite side, slightly higher than the first and angling down to it; it will be this cut that fells the tree. If necessary fit long ropes to higher branches to help guide the tree down, making sure that the ropes are longer than the falling tree.

If a **large branch** has to be lopped, take care not to rip the bark. The free end of the branch should be roped to a branch higher up the tree. Before getting down to the main sawing job, take as much weight off the branch as possible by trimming off its smaller branches. Undercut the limb about 300 mm (12 in) from the trunk, and then cut from above to sever the branch. Lower it to the ground, then untie the outer end. Finally, with a neat single cut, **trim the stub** as close to the trunk as possible.

REMOVING DEAD TREE ROOTS

roots of dead trees (especially large ones) should be removed
from the garden. If they are left in the ground, disease and rot
will set in and this could quite easily affect trees and plants in
other parts of the garden. If the tree is being felled, make sure
that enough of the stump is left to provide adequate leverage for
root removal. Dig a trench around the tree in order to expose
the main root system. Sever the big roots with an axe or bow
saw, and then rock the stump to snap the minor roots. To finish
the job, lever the stump over onto its side and cut the tap root, if
there is one.

If the stump has been cut to ground level, the job can be
tackled in the same way, but is far more difficult. There is a
special machine available that will grind the root out, but this
can be expensive. Alternatively, bore holes about 300 mm
(12 in) deep in the stump and insert one of the **root-killing
chemicals.** Plug the holes very securely with mortar as these
chemicals are *highly poisonous*. The chemical will gradually
kill all growth in the stump, making it easier to remove later.

Dig around stump to
expose main roots

Sever main roots
with saw or axe

68 **FRUIT CAGE** This can be a real boon, protecting crops on
bushes and small trees against the depredations of birds. Mark
out the ground plan of the cage and drive stout poles securely
into the ground at 2 m (6½ in) intervals around the
circumference. Join the poles with a shallow trench (except
between the two that will form the entrance) and fix tightly
stretched wire between all the post tops. Fit plastic netting over
the frame. When the netting is positioned in the trench, the
latter is backfilled; finally, the netting is tied to posts and
overhead wire with rot-proof string.

Staple wire to pole tops

Tie plastic netting to wire and poles

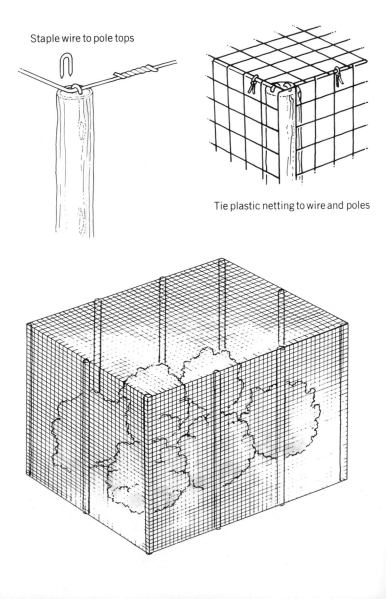

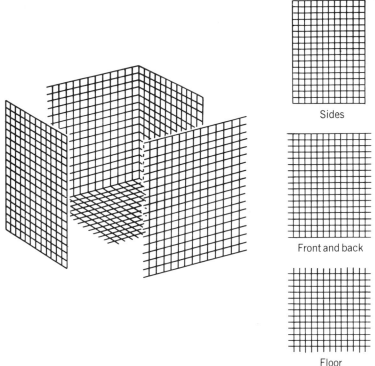

Sides

Front and back

Floor

INCINERATOR A simple but efficient incinerator can be made from five rectangles of heavy-duty wire mesh. The floor measures 650 x 650 mm (26 x 26 in) and the sides, back, and front measure 650 x 900 mm (26 x 36 in). Fit the floor, 150 mm (6 in) above the ground, to horizontal wires on the sides; then fit the front and back.

COMPOST BIN A neat circular compost bin can be made from heavy plastic garden mesh. Mark out a circle 700 mm (28 in) in diameter and dig it out to a depth of 150 mm (6 in). Drive a 50 x 50 mm (2 x 2 in) stake into the ground at a point on the circumference and position the mesh so that it exactly fits the hole; the ends of mesh should overlap by 150 mm (6 in). Tie overlap to the stake with rot-proof string and backfill the hole.

LARGE COMPOST HEAP Compost is invaluable material for the garden, but a large heap of decomposing vegetation makes a rather ugly sight. For this reason, and also because it needs to be out of strong sunlight and cold winds, you will probably want to screen your compost heap. A suitable size for a compost heap when completed is 2 x 1 m (6½ x 3¼ft) and about 1 m (3¼ft) high. First, mark out the area with line and pegs and **dig it out** to a depth of 150 mm (6 in). Put the topsoil on one side, as you will need it for intermediate layers when building the heap. Place a 75 mm (3 in) layer of broken **hardcore** in the dug area, and top this with a layer of **chopped brushwood.** This base will aid both ventilation and drainage. To make a neat heap, you can make a container from interlocking planks, as shown here.

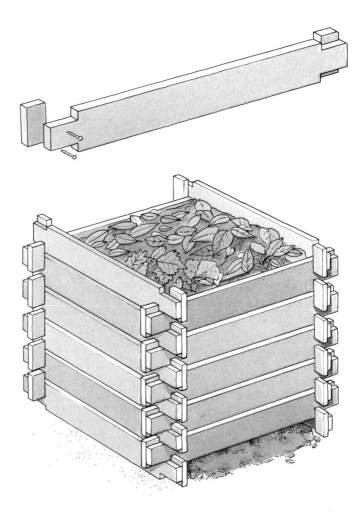

TRAINING CLIMBERS

Climbing plants grown against a wall can be supported with horizontal wires and vine eyes (available at garden centres). Make sure that they are the type with rounded heads rather than sharp square ones, since the latter can inflict a nasty wound to the head of a child running too close. Drill the wall to accept plastic plugs, starting with the bottom row 900 mm (3 ft) above the ground. The holes should be 900 mm (3 ft) apart, and in brickwork make sure that you drill into brick rather than into the pointing. The vine eyes are now screwed into the plastic plugs, and the wires – **galvanised** or **plastic coated** – are threaded through the eyes. The wires should be spaced at 450 mm (18 in) intervals up the wall. The height of your topmost wire will depend on what plants you are training; many climbers easily top a 5 m (16½ ft) wall.

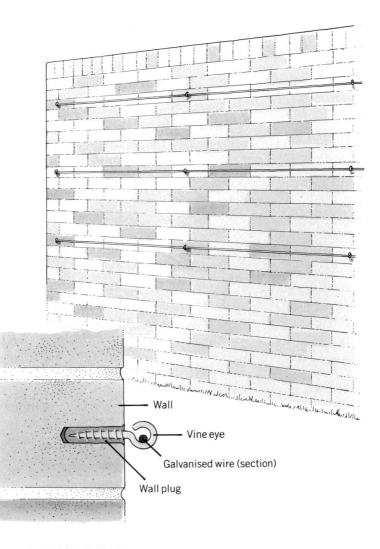

Wall

Vine eye

Galvanised wire (section)

Wall plug

FRUIT STORAGE Fruit needs to be stored in a dry, well-ventilated atmosphere, free from frost and other climatic extremes. A loft is *not* the ideal place to store fruit.

A storage **cabinet,** on the other hand, can take up minimal space, whether standing on the floor or even hung from secure battens on the wall of any suitable room. Keep construction of the frame as simple as possible, using the tray runners to fix the four main uprights together as shown in the drawing. The sides can be left open and suitably braced, or they may be closed with ply or blockboard, when they offer useful hanging surfaces in storeroom or workshop. Ventilation is provided by slatted trays and slatted top, which allow air to drift between and past each fruit. The trays should be approximately 50 mm (2 in) deep and be spaced 50 mm (2 in) apart. A 10-tray cabinet should be capable of holding up to 30 kg (66 lb) of fruit.

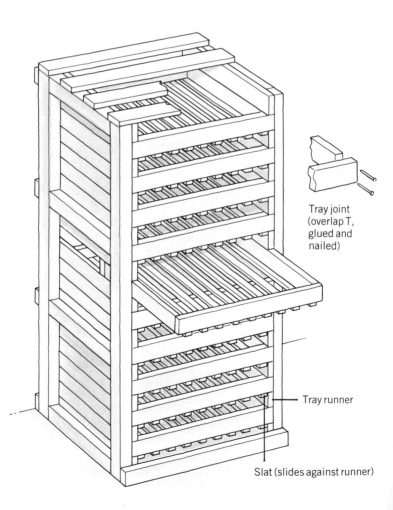

Tray joint
(overlap T,
glued and
nailed)

Tray runner

Slat (slides against runner)

STORING CHEMICALS

The safe storage of garden chemicals, especially insecticides, herbicides, and fungicides, is absolutely essential if you have young children around the house. Always keep these chemicals and other materials in clearly labelled bottles.

One way of lessening the dangerous possibilities of these chemicals is to keep them safely in a sturdy cabinet fitted with hasps and padlocks. The cabinet, incidentally, should be positioned out of reach of toddlers, some of whom can work wonders with keys. A suitable cupboard can use simple dowel-and-rebate construction, all joints being pinned and glued. The wood for the ends could be 25 mm (1 in), for shelves and partition 15 mm (1/2 in), while for the back and doors you can use blockboard or ply. The shelves can be fitted on studs, and the whole unit screwed firmly to the wall.

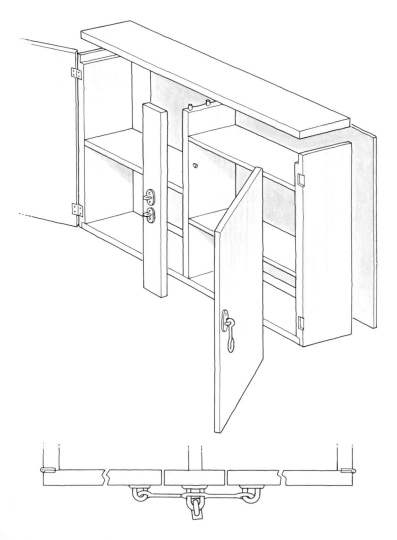

MOWING MACHINES A lawn mower – even an unpowered machine, of which many are still sold – is one of the larger financial investments of the amateur gardener and it makes sense to use and maintain it properly.

As far as unpowered machines are concerned, the correct adjustment of the cutting cylinder is vital. If there is a gap between it and the bottom blade the grass will be torn and ripped out rather than cut cleanly; if the fit is too tight, however, the mower will be difficult to push. Methods of adjusting the cylinder vary from model to model, but they usually involve turning a screw or bolt, either with tools or by hand. When correctly adjusted the blades should be able to cut a stiff piece of paper across the full width of the cylinder. Apart from this, maintenance is minimal and chiefly involves lubricating all moving parts and wiping surfaces with an oily rag after use.

A **cylinder motor mower** revolves the blades at high speed. A stone can do considerable damage, bending or even breaking one of the blades. If bent, a blade can often be tapped straight; but the cylinder as a whole may have been knocked out of shape, and this may mean that part of the blades will miss the bottom cutting edge altogether, producing a ridge in the sward.

It pays dividends to use wire wool or emery paper on the blades from time to time; this removes any rust and slight burrs. Regrinding of the blades is best left to a professional. (If you wish to keep the machine at home, remember to take both the cylinder and the bottom blade to the blade grinder; they work as a matched pair.)

General maintenance will include lubrication. Remove the chain case to reach the chains, and if necessary carry out adjustments to these according to instructions in the maintenance manual. Check that sprockets are correctly aligned and that rollers and all parts run freely.

As far as **petrol engines** are concerned, sparking plugs should always be kept clean. This applies particularly to two-stroke engines which quickly build up carbon deposits. Clean the plug electrodes with fine emery paper, and set the gap with a feeler gauge according to the manual. Plugs should not need to be replaced more than once every two or three years. Change the engine oil regularly, according to the maker's recommendations, as this will help to reduce wear.

The method of winter storage is most important. All petrol should be removed from the engine. Remove the fuel line and drain the tank down, then start the engine and let it run dry. If this is not done, the carburettor jets may become blocked.

Moisture is the enemy of engines, so keep the machine as dry as possible. Turn the engine until it is on the compression

stroke. This closes both the valves and the points and will help
to prevent the entry of damp and the formation of
condensation within the cylinder.

Battery-operated machines need regular topping up and
the battery always needs to be in a good state of charge. Check
all cables and plugs on **mains-operated machines.**

Rotary machines need similar mechanical maintenance to
cylinder mowers. As the rotary blade revolves at very high
speed it tends to become burred and dented. These
irregularities can be carefully filed out. When cutting rough
areas, which are ideal for a rotary, stones, chippings, and
general dirt often get flung against the casing. Wire-brush the
dirt off once a year and apply a car underseal compound.

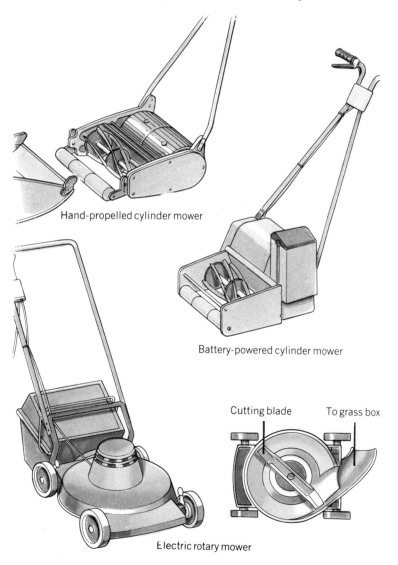

Hand-propelled cylinder mower

Battery-powered cylinder mower

Cutting blade   To grass box

Electric rotary mower

HAND TOOLS While perhaps the most expensive, mowers are only one of a whole range of tools that we use in the garden. Many of these are hand tools that are employed for basic cultivation, and they will need regular care if they are to last long and remain efficient. **Spades** and **shovels** must be kept clean and rust free. A rub down with wire wool followed by regular applications of oil with a rag will keep corrosion at bay. Handles and shafts should be checked for wear and renewed as necessary; the tines of forks and rakes need periodic straightening.

Shears should be kept sharp, oiled, and adjusted. A few strokes with a file will keep the cutting edges at their best; an occasional re-grind by a professional may also be necessary. **Secateurs** need to be oiled; pay particular attention to the spring that ensures smooth operation.

Most **hand saws** can be set and sharpened as necessary – a rather laborious but reasonably simple job. Bow-saw blades cannot be satisfactorily sharpened at home, and it is worth buying new blades for them from time to time. The big old cross-cut saws used for tree felling have now been replaced by **chain saws,** and these can be used to cut virtually any timber.

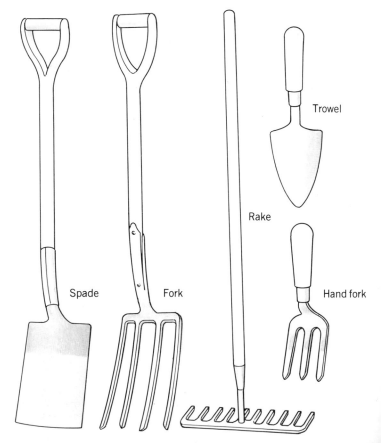

Trowel

Rake

Spade

Fork

Hand fork

General maintenance is similar to that for a 2-stroke mower; remember that it is essential to keep the sparking plug clean. To sharpen a chain saw without the proper tools is virtually impossible. You will need a jig attachment that clamps over the blade. This is used in conjunction with a special file that is drawn across each blade in turn at an angle set by the jig. Always make sure the chain is tensioned correctly; if it is much too loose it could fly off the bar when the saw is in use and could cause serious injuries.

All petrol-engined **cultivators, leaf collectors, edgers,** and other tools will need maintenance as prescribed in the appropriate manuals. Pay particular attention to oil changes and the cleaning of air filters. Contrary to what might be supposed, the garden is a dirty place for machinery. **Electric tools,** too, need careful attention, especially to plugs and cables; the blades of **hedge trimmers** also need regular oiling if they are to give satisfactory service.

As a final point, always use a tool for the job it was intended for and do not tackle work that is beyond the capacity of the machine: at best it would simply mean a job done inefficiently; at worst it could lead to expensive disaster.

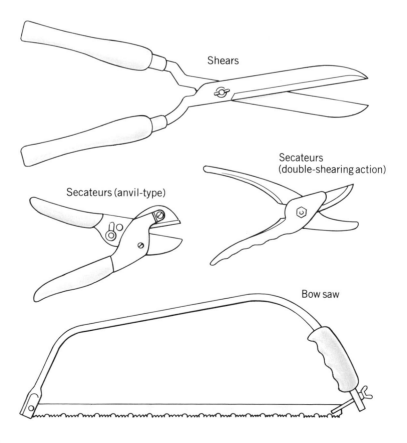

Shears

Secateurs (double-shearing action)

Secateurs (anvil-type)

Bow saw

PERGOLA Although it can be an attractive focal point in the garden, a pergola needs careful siting if its effect is not to appear contrived. It can form a splendid link between different levels of the garden, or it can frame a view.

Although a pergola can vary widely in size, depending on the size of the garden, it should always be well above head height, 2.25 m (7½ ft) being a minimum. The width should be similar or very little less, otherwise the whole structure will look out of proportion. An all-timber construction using western red cedar or other suitably treated softwood is ideal.

Posts should be of 100 mm (4 in) square section, or of a similar diameter if you are using rustic timber. They can either be set in concrete or slid into a land drain that acts as a sleeve. The joints should be simple overlaps fixed with galvanised nails or brass screws.

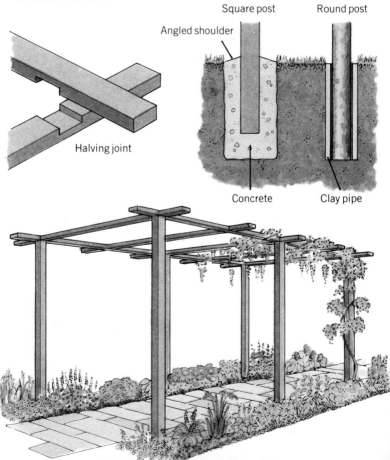

Halving joint

Square post

Angled shoulder

Round post

Concrete

Clay pipe

OVERHEAD BEAMS

While a pergola is free-standing, parallel overhead beams extend out from a house or wall, casting light shade when clothed with climbers and providing a feeling of enclosure that can be delightful in an 'outside room'. As they adjoin a building, they are essentially an architectural feature and their construction should reflect this. Floor joists measuring 225 x 50 mm (9 x 2 in) are ideal, and they should be supported on galvanised hangers fitted into the wall. The front of the beams can be linked together with a similar piece of timber and supported at either side by scaffold poles. These are plugged and a double-ended screw fixed between the dowel and the beams; alternatively, you can use square-section steel tube. The poles or tubes can be painted black and beams painted white, or stained, or sealed. The poles should be sunk at last 900 mm (3 ft) into a concrete foundation, and an area of soil should be left uncovered in a paved area to accommodate climbers. Roofing the structure in corrugated plastic is *not* a good idea; it will collect debris and, although it offers you some protection against light showers, it drums like thunder when it rains hard.

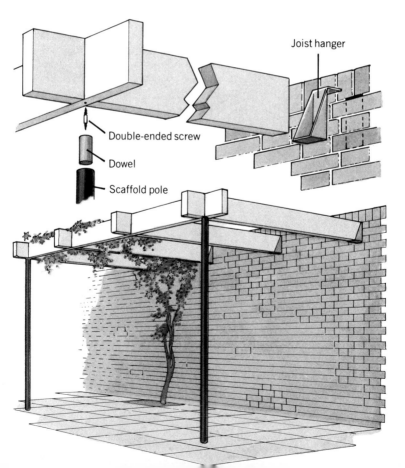

Joist hanger

Double-ended screw

Dowel

Scaffold pole

GARDEN FURNITURE Chairs, tables, and other garden furniture are important in the way they bring purpose and life to your outside room. They are, however, very expensive to buy, and there seem to be remarkably few interesting designs other than the pleasant but ubiquitous white-painted cast aluminium posing as antique-style wrought iron. So why not try your hand at some ideas in timber?

We illustrate a number of designs, all of which are simple enough to be modified to fit your own personal requirements. One of the most important attributes of much garden furniture – and one flatly contradicted by heavy wrought iron – is that it can be moved easily and quickly, outside for guests arriving unannounced, and inside to escape from a cloudburst. If it can serve a secondary purpose, such as storage, so much the better, and one of these designs does just that. This same basic unit doubles as both table or chairs, while the idea of having boldly painted pictures on the back and seat gives the children a chance to contribute to the production.

The conventional table and chair designs are slightly more sophisticated, but still well within the capacity of most do-it-yourself enthusiasts. They could, in fact, be made even simpler with an external-quality plywood table-top and with moulded-ply seats for the chairs. They are light in weight, and the table could easily be made large enough to seat four people comfortably. The chair frame, including cross braces, is made up of 50 x 25 mm (2 x 1 in) section softwood, with a 75 x 25 mm (3 x 1 in) backrest. The top slats of the table could be of 125 x 25 mm (5 x 1 in) softwood, and the frame of 50 x 25 mm (2 x 1 in) softwood. The coach bolts will need to be at least 65 mm (2½ in) long.

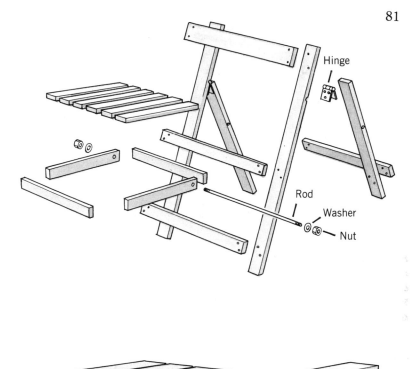

Hinge

Rod

Washer

Nut

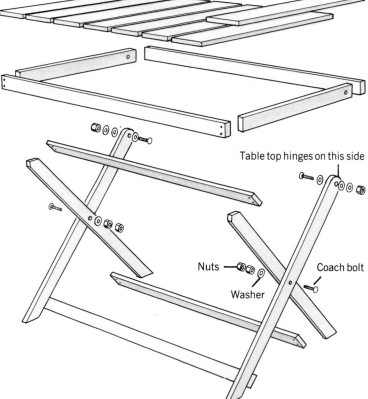

Table top hinges on this side

Nuts

Washer

Coach bolt

82 SEAT/TABLE/STORE

This piece of furniture is simple enough in design and construction for even the least experienced do-it-yourselfer. The material for the top and bottom is 20 mm (¾ in) exterior-grade plywood; the sides can be of the same material or softwood. The height is about 225 mm (9 in); the top is about 1 m (3¼ ft) square, and overhangs the sides by 25 mm (1 in) all round. Make the top in two hinged sections so that the smaller section forms a seat back that can be folded flat when not in use. When raised it is held in place at a reclining angle by battens. Finish the exposed edges of the ply with hardwood strip. All joints should be glued and screwed. Before assembly, treat all internal surfaces and the bottom with preservative. Fill screw holes and sand down external surfaces before painting with primer, undercoat, and top coat.

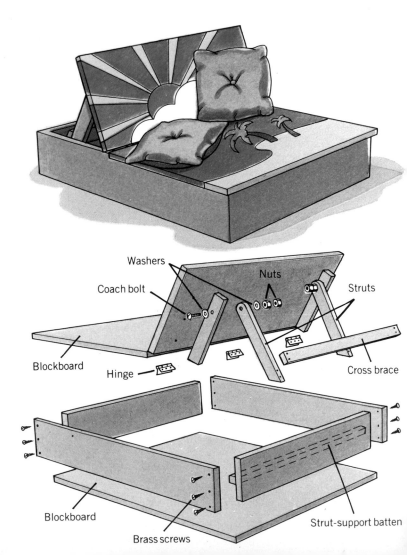

Washers

Nuts

Coach bolt

Struts

Blockboard

Hinge

Cross brace

Blockboard

Strut-support batten

Brass screws

TREE SEAT

Just as a tree can act as a pivot for an entire scheme, so a seat built around its base can form the heart of a large, shady sitting area. To make this a worthwhile piece of furniture, both the tree and the seat need to be of ample size, the latter measuring a minimum of 2 m (6½ ft) square. The seat thus becomes something more – perhaps doubling as a table or even as a lounger. Construction should be in robust lengths of softwood – perhaps 225 x 25 mm (9 x 1 in) planks for the top – leaving ample space around the trunk to allow for movement in a high wind; if the tree is still in vigorous growth, room should also be allowed for the trunk's expansion. If the area around the tree is to be paved, make sure that water from the paving drains *towards* the tree bole, rather than away from it. Finish the seat either with a preservative or with a primer, undercoat, and exterior-quality gloss topcoat.

50 x 50 mm (2 x 2 in) supports for planking

75 x 25 mm (3 x 1 in) batten

75 x 75 mm (3 x 3 in) legs

SUN LOUNGER We have said that garden furniture should if possible be portable; but, of course, the larger the piece the more of a problem this is likely to be. Sun loungers, however, are both attractive in appearance and thoroughly practical since you can move them around the garden in order to follow the sun. Their wheels and legs also allow you to bask clear of damp ground, an important consideration in our variable climate. The 'mattress' and back-support cushion can be made out of foam rubber with fitted fabric covers.

The lounger shown here is constructed of softwood and has a removable backrest that allows it to be easily stored when not in use. The main framework and the slats for the top and backrest are all made from the same-sized timber, 125 x 25 mm (5 x 1 in); this simplifies both ordering and assembly. The joints are straightforward, and the thing to remember about the wheels is that they should be large enough to enable you to push the lounger easily over long or wet grass.

After assembling the timber, mark out and cut all components to size. On the backrest slats and the main framework use mortice-and-tenon or box joints for strength, fixing them with exterior-quality wood glue. One handle can be marked out with a cardboard template and cut to size with a coping saw; then you can use this finished handle as a template for marking out the second. The backrest slots can be made from offcuts and should be glued and screwed into position. The slots will, of course, need to be set at an angle to the vertical. Those nearer the handles, for the sitting position, should be somewhat more upright than those for the lounging position. Use substantial screws when fixing the slots to the main framework: they will have to withstand considerable pressure when the lounger is in use. The legs should be 75 x 75 mm (3 x 3 in), tenons being cut inside the front pair to accept the wheels; the latter can be held in position with threaded axle bolts, using nuts and washers.

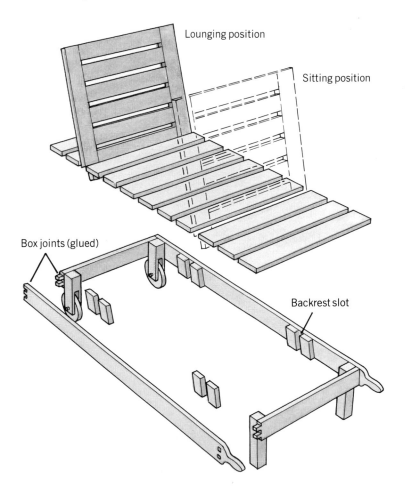

Lounging position

Sitting position

Box joints (glued)

Backrest slot

TREE HOUSE For those who have a large and suitably accommodating tree, tree houses are fun. Some of the most successful examples have an impromptu look about them: they should be able to be made quickly and easily; they should be simple enough to be made by young carpenters using basic techniques, albeit under the supervision of an adult; and while they must be strong and safe, they should not strive too hard to achieve the over-neat appearance that an adult might like but that many children would find boring. Make sure, before building begins, that the tree in question is strong enough to

carry both the house and numerous agile bodies comfortably and securely. For reasons of both safety and sound horticulture, check the tree for any dead wood, and remove it.

The framework should consist of 75 x 50 mm (3 x 2 in) or, better, 100 x 50 mm (4 x 2 in) softwood, suitably treated with a preservative or painted with wood primer, undercoat, and topcoat. It is perfectly adequate to use simple joints, such as halving joints that are glued and screwed together. **Crossbraces** in the same-sized timber can be positioned as necessary; an exterior-grade ply is suitable for the **top.** Once the platform is in position you must bore holes in the crossbraces or siderails to accept the **ropes** that will bind the structure to the branches or trunk. Offcuts can be used as **stabilising blocks** to make the floor horizontal, and these should be nailed to the tree.

A **canvas awning,** slung from the branches above, will keep off showers and provide shade, while access can be by a **knotted rope** or a rope ladder at least 15 mm (½ in) thick. Make a particular point of ensuring that at least one of the ropes binding the structure to the tree is positioned immediately opposite the access rope or ladder.

Two 6 mm (¼ in) nylon ropes at each binding point

75 x 50 mm (3 x 2in) stabilising block nailed to tree

Exterior-grade plywood glued and screwed to frame

Halving joint, glued and screwed

100 x 50 mm (4 x 2 in) frame

SUN BLINDS Whether in bright golds and greens or in deliberately 'synthetic-looking' colours, sun blinds give a delightfully cheerful feeling of summer, even if the weather is unrelenting. The blinds shown here are light and simply constructed. They are constructed from canvas or other material stretched over timber frames, and can be folded against the house wall when not in use. They are easily removable at the end of the season.

The **four frames** are identical in size and are made from 40 mm x 25 mm (1½ x 1 in) prepared softwood. Simple butt joints are used at the corners, but these can be strengthened with plywood offcuts, shaped accordingly.

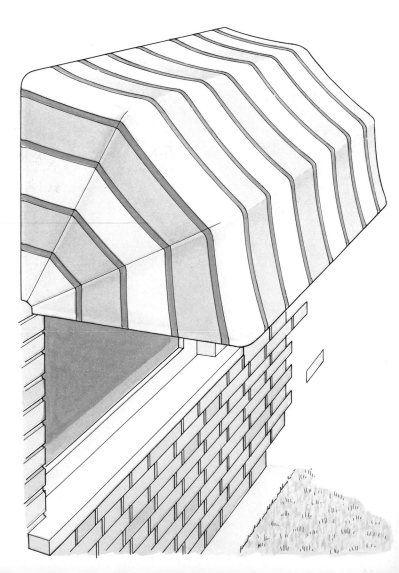

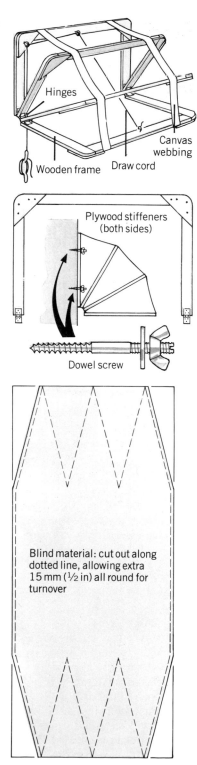

Hinges

Canvas webbing

Wooden frame   Draw cord

Plywood stiffeners
(both sides)

Dowel screw

Blind material: cut out along
dotted line, allowing extra
15 mm (½ in) all round for
turnover

Each frame is backflap-hinged to the one behind, the top (or innermost) frame being fixed to the wall. **Dowel screws** (although you may have to shop around for them) are ideal for this, the wall being drilled and fitted with plastic plugs to accept them. The outer, threaded ends of the dowel screws will project through specially drilled holes in the top frame, and butterfly nuts will hold it in position. (When you wish to take the sun blind down before the onset of winter, all you will need to do is to unscrew the butterfly nuts and pull the innermost frame off the screws.) The frames are joined by **webbing,** and a cord, run through screw eyes in each frame to a **cleat,** draws the blind up.

To make the cover it is best to complete the frame and temporarily fix it near ground level. If you lay the material over the frame you will see that **wedge-shaped sections** need cutting out at the ends, and these should be marked accordingly (a hardboard template can be useful for this operation). Finally, pin the canvas to the outsides and top of the frames with rustproof upholstery nails.

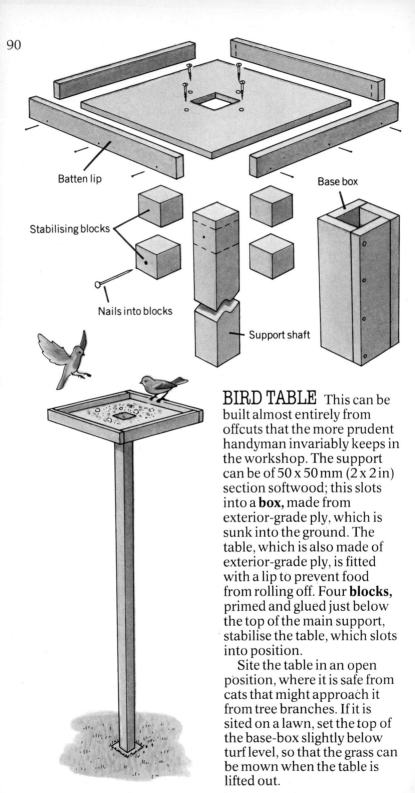

Batten lip

Base box

Stabilising blocks

Nails into blocks

Support shaft

BIRD TABLE This can be built almost entirely from offcuts that the more prudent handyman invariably keeps in the workshop. The support can be of 50 x 50 mm (2 x 2 in) section softwood; this slots into a **box,** made from exterior-grade ply, which is sunk into the ground. The table, which is also made of exterior-grade ply, is fitted with a lip to prevent food from rolling off. Four **blocks,** primed and glued just below the top of the main support, stabilise the table, which slots into position.

Site the table in an open position, where it is safe from cats that might approach it from tree branches. If it is sited on a lawn, set the top of the base-box slightly below turf level, so that the grass can be mown when the table is lifted out.

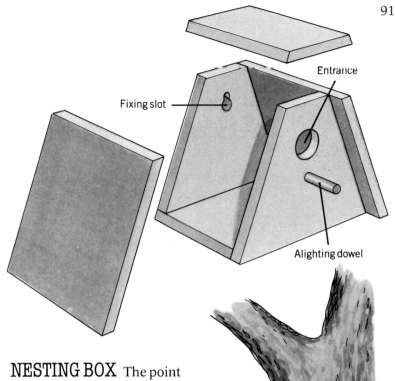

Fixing slot

Entrance

Alighting dowel

NESTING BOX The point to note about a nesting box such as this one is that, within certain limits, you can determine the size of the birds that will use it by the diameter of the entrance hole. The minimum size, so far as British garden birds are concerned, is about 25 mm (1 in) in diameter, which is suitable for the smaller tits. Immediately below the hole insert an alighting bar; dowelling is ideal for this. Exterior-grade plywood offcuts are perfectly suitable material. The box illustrated is 225 mm (9 in) high and the same width at the base. Bore the access hole about 65 mm (2½ in) from the top, and cut a slot in the back wall for fixing. Pin and glue the pieces together, finally applying paint or varnish to the exterior only.

92 HUTCH

Owing to the bewildering variety of pets kept by British families, it is impossible to lay down the law about the size of a typical home-made hutch. In broad terms it must be large enough for the pet to be comfortable, should have both a living and a sleeping compartment, and should be fitted with access doors to both of these to make cleaning straightforward. The roof should be sloped to shed water easily, and wire mesh or netting should always be strong and secure, as animal teeth can quickly make a hole. Do not overlook the possibility of adding an outside run, accessible by a ramp, to one end of the hutch. A run along the front of the hutch can also be useful. The framework should have T halving joints, screwed and glued. The walls, roof, and floor can be constructed from exterior ply.

The RSPCA can supply suitable hutch dimensions for any pet.

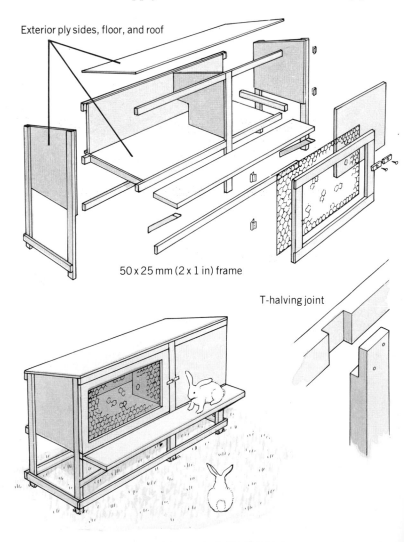

Exterior ply sides, floor, and roof

50 x 25 mm (2 x 1 in) frame

T-halving joint

GARDEN SWING

The **uprights** are cut from prepared 225 x 50 mm (9 x 2 in) softwood. The **top rail** and the **seat** are of 150 x 50 mm (6 x 2 in) softwood. The **beam,** from which the seat is suspended, is of 100 x 50 mm (4 x 2 in) and is set on edge into slots cut into the tops of the uprights. The beam is drilled and fitted with stout eye bolts, nuts, and washers to attach the chains. The uprights are 2.75 m (9 ft) long; they are set 600 mm (2 ft) in the ground and **concreted** in position 1.05 m (41 in) apart.

The seat should be about 550 mm (22 in) long and is drilled to accept eye bolts. A steel strip is drilled to locate with the bolts, and washers should be used under the nuts. Proprietary **nylon chain and shackles** or **nylon rope** can be used to hang the seat from the top rail. Check all parts regularly for safety.

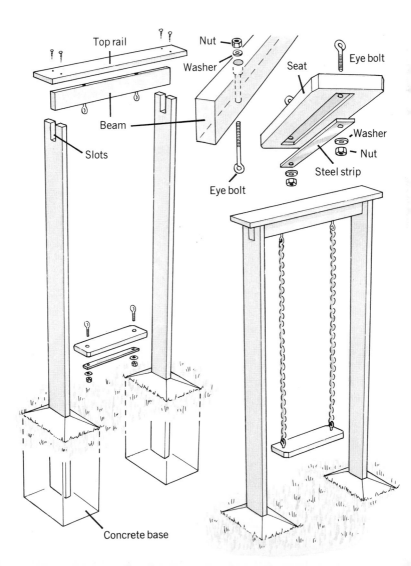

94 SEESAWS

Perhaps even more than swings, seesaws get all kinds of treatment, so they need to be especially tough. Floor joists measuring 225 x 50 mm (9 x 2 in) in section which have been planed all round make ideal seats and the design shown uses these as well for the upright supports for the pivot. The supports must be sunk into concrete, a bottom piece giving added strength. Two beams of 100 x 50 mm (4 x 2 in) section running beneath the seat prevent undue whip, while simple handholds prevent children being thrown off too easily. The seesaw pivots on a circular-section steel bar that runs through carefully aligned screw eyes; pins passing through the legs and above the steel bar allow the seat to be removed when it is not in use. Make sure all surfaces are sanded smooth and painted with a primer, undercoat, and exterior-quality topcoat.

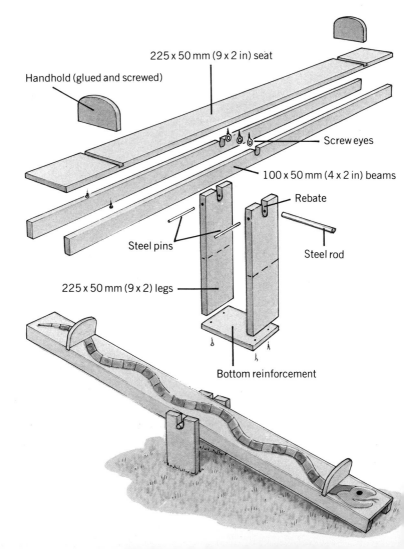

225 x 50 mm (9 x 2 in) seat

Handhold (glued and screwed)

Screw eyes

100 x 50 mm (4 x 2 in) beams

Rebate

Steel pins

Steel rod

225 x 50 mm (9 x 2) legs

Bottom reinforcement

PLAY SLIDE

The advantage of this slide is that it can be dismantled for easy storage. As with the swing, seesaw, and tree house, be sure to supervise its use by young children.

The steps are built with a mortice-and-tenon construction of joints. One side of it can be filled in with a blackboard or simply a rectangle of brightly painted exterior-grade ply. A rug thrown over the top will speedily convert it into a tent or tunnel. The slide is made from 20 mm (¾ in) thick exterior ply not less than 500 mm (20 in) wide; the hand rails that help to stiffen the slide are of 75 x 25 mm (3 x 1 in) section, and the rails and timber 'hook' at the top are securely glued and screwed to the ply. Total length of the slide surface is about 2.5 m (100 in). Smooth all surfaces, paying particular attention to the slide and hand rails, and treat with preservative. Fill all holes, and polish.

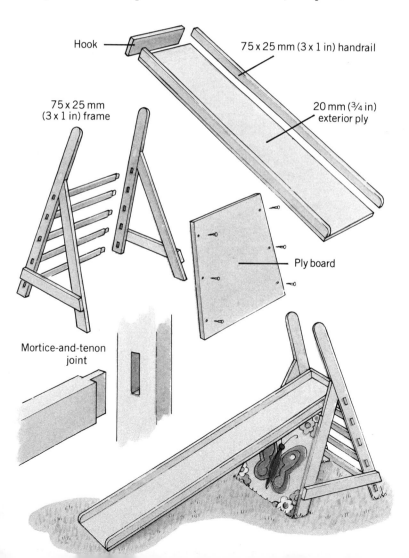

Hook

75 x 25 mm (3 x 1 in) handrail

75 x 25 mm (3 x 1 in) frame

20 mm (¾ in) exterior ply

Ply board

Mortice-and-tenon joint